You Can Control Your Anger!
21 Ways To Do It

Bill Borcherdt, ACSW, BCD

Professional Resource Press
Sarasota, Florida

Published by Professional Resource Press
(An imprint of Professional Resource Exchange, Inc.)
Post Office Box 15560
Sarasota, FL 34277-1560

The copy editor for this book was Patricia Rockwood, the typesetter was Denise Franck, the managing editor was Debra Fink, the production coordinator was Laurie Girsch, and Jami's Graphic Design created the cover.

Library of Congress Cataloging-in-Publication Data

Borcherdt, Bill.
    You can control your anger! : 21 ways to do it / Bill Borcherdt.
        p. cm.
    Includes bibliographical references.
    ISBN 1-56887-061-2 (alk. paper)
    1. Anger. 2. Rational-emotive psychotherapy. I. Title.

RC569.5.A53 B67 2000
616.89'14--dc21

00-028078

Dedication

*To my good friend
Dennis Hahnemann -
a fighter if there ever was one.*

Other books by Bill Borcherdt
Available from
Professional Resource Press
P.O. Box 15560
Sarasota, FL 34277-1560

Think Straight! Feel Great!
21 Guides to Emotional Self-Control

You Can Control Your Feelings!
24 Guides to Emotional Well-Being

Head Over Heart in Love:
25 Guides to Rational Passion

Feeling Right When Things Go Wrong

Publisher's Note

Table of Contents

Introduction

Practically all problems of emotional disturbance are coated in anger. The anger pie, which often ends up being thrown in one's own, others', and/or the world's face, can be cut into three pieces:

1. *Anger at self.* When you err and blame yourself for your blunder, you create self-anger. This is often followed by the misuse of this antagonistic feeling through further self-beratement, for example: "What a bad person I am for acting badly," or "What an idiot I am for acting like a dunce." Because a self-labeled fool, dunce, or idiot cannot learn from his or her mistakes, continued failure is likely to reinforce this view of self as a totally deficient human being. Consequently, self-defeating actions are likely to be multiplied to accommodate this self-as-worthless image. A depressed client purposefully quit his part-time enjoyable, successful avocation of playing in a band because he didn't think that he deserved pleasures in life. He had made himself angry at himself for his shortcomings and then began to pounce upon himself emotionally and behaviorally even more because he believed that self-punishment was what he deserved. He wrongly assumed that somehow, via his self-damnation and torture, he would be better able to correct himself in the future.

Self-anger only creates a double whammy, a multiplying effect that occurs when you not only get after your mistake, but get after yourself for making it. Such self-depreciation leaves you not only with the practical problems of picking up the pieces and going on in life in spite of your errors, but also with the excess emotional anger baggage that will likely hold you back rather than push you forward. It would be far better to concentrate on making fewer errors in the future than to condemn yourself in the present for your original mistake as well as for your deficient coping skills in (mis)managing yourself in the aftermath of such emotional upheaval.

2. *Anger at others.* When others trespass on your values and you berate them you produce anger at those who do not act in accordance with your view of the world. Interpersonal misuse of anger is seen in such hostility-producing ideas as "What a wicked person he/she is for acting wickedly"; "What a rotten person he is to be judged for acting rottenly"; "What a scum my associate is for acting putridly"; or "How bad she is for acting badly." Anger at others encourages passive or not-so-passive actions toward the wrongdoer. This creates an escalating, pyramiding effect in that not only do you have the relationship problems of difficulty blending into the flow of the other's attack, but you must also cope with the excess burden and baggage of taking anger along into the dispute or feud. You might experience better emotional gain by using the strained aspects of the relationship to work on your own mental health via building a case for tolerance, acceptance, and forgiveness of the wrongdoer while (unangrily) protecting yourself from the other person (i.e., create a temporary distance between you and the unruly, misbehaving opposition).

3. *Anger at life and/or the universe.* When the world doesn't devote itself to making you happy, it is no time to take a bad situation and make it worse. When life is seemingly

being its typical unbiased self while refusing to give you the benefit of the doubt, it is the best time to be fair to yourself by (unangrily) not taking these difficult circumstances and multiplying them. When life inconveniences you and you magnify the significance of such oversights, demanding that such randomness not exist, you will make yourself angry as witnessed by you walking around with a chip glued to your shoulder. Here too, double jeopardy is created in that you will not only be looking for remedies to close the gap between what you're wanting in life and what you're getting, but you will also carry with you self-defeating grudges, resentments, and animosities that will bog you down in seeking the advantages that you desire. Ideas such as "Life sucks," "How terrible life is for treating me terribly," and "How horrid life is for treating me so undesirably" bring out bitterness toward the universe. It would be better to understand and accept the random, impartial, neutral nature of life than to protest against its shortcomings. All things, for better or for worse, that occur in life should occur because they do. To angrily deny this fact of life clashes with reality, with reality winning out.

Anger is a comprehensive problem that exhausts personal and interpersonal happiness the world over. As an unhealthy emotion it is misused more than perhaps all of the other interfering emotions put together (i.e., anxiety, fear, worry, guilt, and depression). The study of its creation and correction has the potential for freeing up redeeming value that contributes to the better emotional interest of individuals, couples, families, groups, and even nations.

The goals of this book are to expose the anatomy and mechanics of this happiness-killing emotion combined with philosophical and practical recommendations that will lighten the anger load. Anger is not caused by pesky, unwanted circumstances, but by one's thinking about one's less-than-desirable observations. Rational Emotive Behavior Therapy (REBT), as created by Albert Ellis, PhD, in 1955, staunchly maintains that it is not the activating adversity at point "A" that causes people to feel anger at point "C" (emotional consequences); it is their thoughts or conclusions about "A" that largely/mainly cause anger. People may be angry *about* the distasteful, triggering event at "A," but REBT holds that individuals are not angered *by* "A," but rather about their thinking about the situation. Further, people can bend their way of thinking and are not required to bend the universe in an effort to not get themselves emotionally bent out of shape (see p. xiii).

This teaching method that intervenes in human thought, feelings, and behaviors is a quick and high-quality way to head off unwanted feelings of anger. A thorough understanding of this method leaves you a means of better disciplining your emotions - regardless of circumstances. By tracking down your anger-producing thoughts at "B" and *d*ebating, *d*isputing them while thinking *d*ifferently at "D" you exercise your capability to better control, if not dissolve, your angry mood while leaving the door open for discovering more healthful emotions that make your life more pleasant. However, giving up anger doesn't mean you don't have feelings - it's just that you are better able to increase your fuller emotional capability once you extinguish anger. This filters into "E" with its new-found *e*ffects, *e*nergy, and *e*ncountering of new-found beliefs/philosophies/conclusions that unangrily break the back of anger by giving up the irrational thoughts that caused it to begin with.

Dr. Ellis is currently the President of The Albert Ellis Institute in New York City. There are now nationally and internationally based Rational Emotive Behavior Therapy Centers, and REBT's cognitive, emotive, and behavioral ideas are practiced by thousands of therapists all over the globe, a good number of whom were trained by Dr. Ellis and his Institute staff. Readers

ILLUSTRATION OF DR. ELLIS'S ABC'S
OF ANGER CONTROL

A (Adversity, activating event)	B (Beliefs)	C (Feelings, emotional consequences)	D (Different way of thinking)	E (New effects, new ways of looking at old problems, healthier emotional outcomes)
You err	"I must not make mistakes and I am a bad person for doing so."	Anger Rage	"I obviously can and have a right to make mistakes."	Determination to reshuffle the cards of life's possibilities, followed by dealing oneself a better hand.
Others err	"Others must not make mistakes and are bad for doing so."	Fury Hostility Resentment Vindictiveness	"Others can and obviously have a right to make mistakes."	Displeasure Annoyance
Life deals you a bad hand	"Life must continually deal me a good hand, and it's bad when it doesn't."	Self-Pity Sulking	"Life can and often will deal me a bad, unfortunate hand."	Irritation

interested in receiving the Institute's semiannual brochure describing its various educational and training seminars and psychoeducational materials (books, pamphlets, posters, audio- and videotapes, etc.) can request one by writing the Institute at 45 East 65th Street, New York, NY 10021.

Anger sadly is at the head of its class in dubious, self-defeating ways. It instigates feuds, conflicts, wars, genocide, nationalism, and domestic violence, all of which have put our species on the brink of destruction. REBT offers a more scientific, civilized approach that makes allowances for imperfections in self, others, and the universe. Before Dr. Ellis invented his revolutionary view that disputed the idea that the stimulus causes the response, humankind was at the mercy of their environment; their "A's" (activating events/adversities) saw no other alternative and as a result thought themselves to be on a shoestring, the plaything of their circumstances (i.e., as one's life circumstances go, so go one's emotions). REBT is a message of hope that points its students in the direction of seeing self as a more active participant in one's emotional problems and disturbance - and in their correction. Long live REBT! Short live anger! Better yet, use REBT principles to prevent angers occurrence.

John F. Kennedy said "The best time to fix the hole in the roof is when the sun is shining." So too, the best time to practice, study, and train against anger's development is before you rain anger in yourself. "Who wouldn't feel angry in the face of unfairness, undeservingness, injustice, and discrimination?" I'm glad you asked - someone in his or her right mind due to the consistent practice of REBT - thats who. As Mark Twain said, "It takes me three weeks to prepare for an impromptu speech." Because of anger's abrupt nature, unshackling yourself from anger requires some rehearsal, that is, talking sense to yourself and visualizing yourself following through with your plan: "The next time I'm disappointed by my, others', and/or life's performances I will tell myself to 'chill out,' 'go easy,' 'lighten up,' 'don't make such a big deal out of it,' and 'give yourself some emotional slack.'"

Before I expose and redefine anger for what it is, I would like to illustrate what it isn't, so that these misunderstandings can be set aside and so that we can more purely highlight anger's reality substance and corrective suggestions.

What Anger Is Not

1. *A frustration or stress reducer.* Contrary to conventional wisdom, anger expression *increases,* not decreases, stress, tension, and frustration. This is because what the angry-acting person is venting his or her frustration toward often doesn't change - especially when it is another person who refuses to change upon the command of the angry party. Frustration mounts as energy is spent but nothing changes. When the angry person expects a return on his or her complaints, but gets none, this further pumps up the frustration quotient. The result is a vicious cycle, wherein (a) anger expression fails to remove frustration, then, (b) this futility multiplies the original stress level, leading to (c) more frantic anger production, resulting in (d) more frustration for coming up short in being unable to change the world and its inhabitants. The cycle continues as the angry participant is unable to fill the bottomless pit of his or her frustrations.

2. *The result of unmet "needs."* People anger themselves because they either invent the notion that they have "needs" or are told by someone that they do and are gullible enough to believe what they hear. When you impose the "unmet needs" theory, you become an accomplice in contributing to the other's emotional disturbance. REBT theory as created by Dr. Ellis maintains that it is your belief that you have "needs" to begin with that trigger anger; after all, if you define that you "need" something from another, for

example, love, approval, understanding, acceptance, communication, and so on, you are likely to swear by and swear
at: swear by the notion that you require certain things
from others, and swear at them when they don't deliver
the alleged necessities. Abolish the "need" and you abolish
the anger.

3. *Depression turned inward.* To the contrary, the angry person can blame another and outwardly produce anger. Depression is often the result of blaming oneself, while anger
is an offshoot of blaming someone else. Depression may
occur following the hopelessness that is felt when you discover that the universe doesn't bend despite your (worst)
best efforts to do so. Being forced to come off the throne of
your stance as general manager of the universe by proxy
can prove to be a helpless, hopeless, feelings-of-futility
experience - sometimes amplified into depression, but not
so at the beginning.

4. *A learned behavior.* A client who physically abused his wife
told me of his father who had beaten his mother. One
would think that the theory that children learn what they
see, or that children are products of their environment,
would obviously come into play in such a like-father-like-
son activity. However, I discovered the not-so-obvious fact
that my client had been raised by his grandparents who
had no history of abuse in their relationship! There are
many examples of children who never saw one or both of
their parents, but yet are like the absentee parent(s). Also,
children are quite selective in what they choose to learn
from their parents. For instance, a typical example would
be a 15-year-old boy who is sent to counsel with me regarding anger and aggressive problems at school. He
might justify his anger by telling me a fact of his upbring-
ing: that his father acted angrily practically every day of
the week and twice on Sundays (the day he was around
more), and that therefore he lays claim to the self-created

theory that he learned his angry antics from his dad. However, as I get to know the young boy more, I will likely discover that he is not a clone of his father. For example, perhaps his dad has not missed a day of work in 20 years, but the young man is skipping school left and right. Like practically all children, this young man is selective in what he decides to imitate in his father. He is born into angry tendencies, rather than those tendencies being born out of his observances of his old man.

5. *A necessity for human motivation.* There are many ways to motivate yourself toward your goals and objectives. Anger is but one - and a self-defeating one at that.

6. *A requirement for opposing oppression.* Use anger to oppose oppression and chances are fair that you will take on the tyrannical, bigoted, dictatorial, fanatical means of your oppressors. Two wrongs don't make a right. Some of the great peace advocators of our time didn't deem anger as a necessity in order to get their point across. Two examples are Martin Luther King and Gandhi.

7. *A healthy emotion.* Annoyance, irritation, displeasure, dissatisfaction: These four emotions are healthy; anger is not in their league. They all result when a wish gets thwarted and you begin to feel a certain amount of frustration leading to these four feeling states. It is only when it is demanded that such frustrations be removed that anger is created.

8. *A safe way to express feelings.* Anger often gets out of hand in the form of feuds, wars, domestic disturbances, and various other types of human harm/killing ways. To say that anger is a safe way to express your disenchantment with life is the equivalent to believing that it's safe to light a firecracker in your hand or to throw gasoline on a bonfire.

9. *An effective way to express feelings/messages.* Speak in anger and you will block others' understanding of what you are attempting to say. Anger is a try-too-hard method that

often results in your message being kept under wraps by the angry fog that surrounds it.

10. *A good way to motivate others.* Anger may get you immediate intimidating results in that in the short run others may scare themselves into giving you what you want, but in the long run your boisterous demands will likely drive them away.

11. *A way to increase a keen and well-rounded state of mind.* Anger eliminates options with its one-sided emotional alliance. Preferences give way to demands due to humans' allergy to them. Tunnel vision destroys alternatives; one and only one way is promoted, and alternative or optional thinking is surrendered in favor of single-mindedness. Consequently, cooperation, collaboration, and comprising possibilities get lost in the angry scuffle.

12. *The result of lack of praise and appreciation.* It is the demand that you be praised, appreciated, and cuddled for that which you do well that ignites anger, not the lack thereof that is the offender. The unfulfillment of a dire "need" for appreciation rests at the base of much anger.

13. *A consequence of observing and/or experiencing injustice, unfairness, and undeservingness.* Here, too, it is not the experience of injustice, and so on that powers and powders anger, but the demand that eminent justice be more the rule, if not THE rule, rather than the exception.

14. *A signature of strength to be admired and revered.* Anger leaves its handwriting in the form of fear, weakness, and insecurity. There is very little to be exalted in the oppositionalism of a 2-year-old.

15. *An emotion that will automatically run its course without any conscious exertion on your part.* Rather, anger feeds upon itself. It will pyramid and build itself into further not-so-great heights if left unattended to be indiscriminately expressed.

16. *An emotion that spontaneously releases itself without prior thought.* This "big bang" theory overlooks the precon-

ceived ideas that humans have about varying circumstances, and when these situations appear, anger is made to let loose, triggered by the irrational, dysfunctional beliefs that preceded it.

17. *An emotion that shows you mean business.* Anger is a mean way to demonstrate to others that the content of your discussions is important to you. Such displays of anger as representing importance will have others abandoning you, being too afraid to stick around to find out what you meant about what you're saying.

18. *A method that keeps you out of harm's way.* On the contrary, anger begets, invites, encourages, and leaves the door wide open for others to levy anger back toward you. Result: More harm getting in the way of reaching your desired ends.

19. *The result of someone's mistakes.* Personalizing or exaggerating the significance of another's blunder will bring on anger, not the goofing itself.

20. *The consequences of neglectful parents.* Despising your parents for not being the only parents in the universe who are without fault will build a case for anger, but this angry aggravation has virtually nothing to do with the facts of the neglect. Rather, it is the continual "the show never ends" insistence that such a reality should not have existed that turns anger's ignition.

21. *The result of dysfunctional past or present interactions with significant others.* Dysfunctional circumstances do not cause emotional disturbance; dysfunctional beliefs about those same transgressions will. Anger or any other emotion is not transmitted interpersonally as many would have you believe. It is the thinking about the past, present, or possible future occurrences that activates emotional upset.

22. *The consequence of unconscious forces such as underlying resentment toward one's parents, usually the mother.* Angry people know what they are feeling and against whom their anger is directed. They may sometimes seem to be

confused about the origin of their wrath, but right near the plight of their anger is a demand directed toward someone or something that does not meet with their favor in the here and now. To analytically search for buried motivation is wasteful when the trigger of the angry occurrence can be quickly uncovered rather than laboriously hunted. Explanatory self-statements that reflect commands, demands, grandiosity, and intolerance can be rapidly identified as the behind-the-scenes creator of the smoking gun called anger.

23. *The end result of media teachings and modeling.* For better or for worse, it is difficult to stifle human potential. Anger is not triggered by aggressive media portrayals. Rather, those who consistently use anger as a life-adjustment style do so because they are predisposed toward doing so - accidents waiting to happen, if you will. They will simply express anger without any imitative, visual aids, and they will do so in many contexts of living that they find frustrating. If you have anger in your bones, you don't require media's assistance in expressing it. Better that you acknowledge these predisposed inclinations and see them as the natural phenomena that they are rather than the imitative substance that they aren't. Then work very hard to contain them lest you yourself end up disposing of self and others.

If anger is *not* all those dastardly things listed above, what is its vile makeup? For a redefinition of the mechanics of this harmful emotion, review the beginning of this introduction, which redefines anger in a way that highlights its intricacies. Keep in mind that anger with a "d" in front of it spells "danger." To respect and avoid anger's redefined danger so as to more favorably experience life is one of the main goals of the following chapters.

At the end of each chapter, you will find a list of review questions related to the content of that chapter. Use the questions as a basis for feedback and discussion in individual or group sessions or simply to remind yourself of key points.

Bill Borcherdt, ACSW, BCD
April, 2000

Introduction Review Questions

1. What are the three directions that anger can be targeted toward?

2. Why is anger an unhealthy emotion?

3. What is Dr. Albert Ellis's ABC model of dealing with anger?

4. What are some of the things that anger isn't?

5. What are some of the mechanics of anger, and which one is most obvious to you?

CHAPTER 1

Anger Redefined - As D/Anger

Anger can be redefined into parcels, each of which can play a part in instigating a full-blown expression of this obnoxious feeling state. Each dimension will now be reviewed as to how it contributes to the overall anatomy of anger's existence. Because of anger's philosophical beginnings, newer, more helpful philosophies will be offered. Without these redefinitions of anger, anger could not continue to flourish and instead would evaporate.

Anger can be redefined as:

1. *Demandingness.* If the angry-acting person were not demanding that someone or something be different than he/she/it is, anger could not be created and sustained. Beginning with a preference and escalating it into a demand manufactures anger abundantly, for example, "I want to obtain my goals, be treated better, make life more convenient, so therefore I must be granted my first choice."
2. *Condemnation.* Anger at a human contains condemning views or else such a hostile, intrusive feeling could not define itself as such.
3. *Punitiveness.* Vengeance and punishment flow from anger and are an integral part of its existence.

4. *An agent of control.* Anger expressions are often a crusty attempt to intimidate and manipulate others to give you what you think you require from them. Without the notion that you need certain things from others - for instance, approval, understanding, acceptance, or love - you would be hard put to spit anger.

5. *Disguised hurt.* Hurt is a feeble, weak feeling that often precedes anger. As anger is made to replace hurt, emotional strength is temporarily established. In the long run it would be better to admit to the hurt so that this crucial element of anger can be identified and extinguished. The result: no hurt, no anger.

6. *An addiction.* At the top of its temper-prone ladder, anger ignites heightened feelings of consciousness that, as with any addiction, feels good in the short run but creates more problems in the long run. The angry-acting person practices a bad, overreactive habit by seeking gratification and indulgence through anger's feel-good, addictive component.

7. *New-found nerve gas, boldness, and assertion.* Angry-acting people often discover that they can more easily motivate themselves to fight unfairness and oppression while more staunchly striving for their personal goals. What they don't realize is that there are other methods to create self-incentive.

8. *An instant enhancer of self-esteem.* While in the throes of anger, its holder feels superior, better than others who think differently than they. These feelings of superiority have a skyrocketing effect on building what is popularly termed self-esteem. Creators of anger not only deem themselves better off for being able to angrily control for what is insisted upon, but also appraise themselves as being better people than those who think differently than they. Such attachments to self-appraisals where you define yourself by your presumed rightness and the other's assumed wrongness have no basis in reality. Far better it would be to

challenge the alleged superiority of your values as well as the notion of yourself as superior.

9. *Fear.* Angry-acting people are often afraid of what they believe you can do to them, for example, demean, disgrace, or insult them, or put them down. Anger provides a convenient protective smoke screen to disguise yet seemingly neutralize the fear factor.

10. *Worry.* Overconcerned over what others might think of them, angry people improvise to insure leaving a strong impression on others. However, jaded attempts to perfume disapproval anxiety usually result in an even more negative backlash from one's social group.

11. *Emotional weakness, not strength.* What you see isn't what you get. Those who produce anger are really little people in big people's pants. Angry-acting people are feeble-acting people who try to hide their psychological wimp insecurities in their sea of anger.

12. *Vulnerability, not invulnerability.* Putting themselves on a shoestring by making themselves vulnerable to your favorable opinion of them and to their successful performances leaves them at the mercy of factors beyond their control.

13. *A poor problem-solving method.* Due to its narrowed focus, anger is anticooperative, anticollaborative, and against compromise. Rather than get themselves to the same side of the table to fight the problem, angry-acting ignited people remain at opposite sides of the table, fighting each other.

14. *Expressional but not remedial.* "Getting it off your chest" methods of expression do not come to terms with how you created this lethal feeling state to begin with. As a result, anger boomerangs - it goes out the back door and comes in the front.

15. *Begetting anger.* A show of anger is an open invitation to others to get themselves angry back at you - and is probably the main consequence of a display of anger.

16. *Bigotry.* Black-or-white, dictatorial, all-or-nothing thinking form the foundation of anger. The fascistic idea that people who possess certain characteristics, traits, and features are better than those who have different ways about them can form the basis for anger.

17. *Intolerance.* Unable to establish a decent respect for individual differences, refusals to accept people and matters as they are press anger into action.

18. *Grandiosity.* The belief that because the world was made for me and that it and those in it must give me whatever I want and see to it that I not get anything that I don't want drives a wedge between demands and reality. Demanding that this grandiose perceptual gap not exist fans rather than douses the flames of anger.

19. *Internally, not externally caused.* Anger is created by your thinking about what you observe, not from the observations themselves. This is probably the most basic hypothesis underlying more rational living.

20. *Fueling, not quelling emotions.* Anger throws gasoline on events; its expression often produces emotional wildfire. Feuds, wars, domestic violence, and endless argumentations are the products of such negative expressions.

21. *An emotional transgression that can be evaporated/dissolved.* Anger's fires can be put out with a change of thinking in the more tolerant, less demanding direction. Getting rid of anger *doesn't* mean getting rid of feelings. Others *will* trespass on your values; you will, if you're honest with yourself, have strong, keen feelings about such trespassing on your rules for living - but they can be contained to the point where you learn to more consistently make yourself feel rationally annoyed, irritated, or displeased without bringing on to yourself irrational anger. Developing a philosophy of "I want what I want, but I don't need what I want" will likely save the life of emotional sanity.

22. *Frustration pyramided into demand.* Just as desire or want is not need, so too frustration is not anger. Deeming it essential that what or whom you are disenchanted about not exist will amplify frustration into anger.

23. *Increasing frustration.* Protesting against unpleasantries has a cumulative frustration effect. This is because most of the things, and people, in life that we disapprove of don't change that much. Therefore, frustration is increased in the form of hooting and howling, moaning and groaning related to expending vast amounts of energy to change targeted people and things - but alas, with little if any return.

24. *The 11th commandment.* Moses forgot about perhaps the most obvious demand en route to bitterness: "My will be done."

25. *The reverse Golden Rule.* Being kind and pleasant toward others doesn't require them to respond back to you with no lapses in such favoritism. To attempt to establish such a universal tradeoff, that "others must do unto me as I do unto them" is to invite angry rebuttal when you discover that others have their own pleasant agenda - that may not include you!

26. *Semantic imprecision, a distorted philosophy of life.* Anger, like all emotions generally, and emotional disturbances specifically, are philosophically based. Using the applied philosophical principles of Rational Emotive Behavior Therapy (REBT) to counter the irrational ideas that generate anger can assist in regulating hostile, angry feelings, for example: "Others can follow their own lead, not my lead, while determining for themselves how they wish to carry themselves in this life."

27. *A protest against reality.* Loosening up frozen judgments while abandoning stubbornness, pigheadedness, and bullheadedness in the process of accepting rather than disclaiming reality neutralizes, if not abolishes, the refusal to

accept the reality core of anger. The jugular vein of anger is severed by taking on this philosophy of undamning acceptance. This philosophy recognizes that everything (including others' undesirable behavior) exists in life and abandons absolutistic inventions to the contrary, for example: "This must not be," "This should be different," and "This has to change."

28. *Autistic navel staring.* Angry-ridden people have themselves all wrapped up in their own right and righteousness. Not being able to see beyond the philosophy of "you for me and me for me," they remain fixed and fixated on their own views. Unable or unwilling to expand their perspective, they anger themselves at anyone who has a contrary view beyond their myopic, tunnel-vision notions. In love with themselves and their ideas leaves them with few rivals.

29. *Overemphasis upon restraint as bad.* Restraint, preferably of the unangry type, is not a dirty word. More problems in the world come from lack of restraint than from holding back interfering emotional expressions. Yet, for many, anger is an emotion that absolutely must be expressed. Defining anger as a feeling state that is required to be expressed leads to domestic and irrational havoc; redefining it as an unhealthy emotion that would be better to restrain prevents unwanted, warlike return whipping occurrences.

30. *A boomerang.* Anger expression will not dissolve anger, getting it out the back door and keeping it there. Rather, anger will return via the front door unless major surgery is done on the irrational thinking that caused the anger to begin with. What does it profit people if they temporarily relieve their anger and then relive it because the irrational notions that have caused it go undetected, unchallenged, and unchanged?

31. *An expression that causes one to feel better but to get worse.* Immediate relief can be had via the anger expres-

sion method. However, you *get worse* in the sense that you rehearse the self-defeating symptom and godlike philosophies behind it. With practice you get better at acting badly!

32. *A dictatorship.* "Thou shalt have no other values besides mine" is the totalitarian philosophy behind the venom of anger.

33. *Fanaticism.* Dogma and fanaticism are probably the greatest problems facing the human condition. Unless confronted directly, they will not go away by themselves. Scientifically speaking, nothing is 100%, but try to convince the true believer that he or she is anything but all correct and you will likely get one big sneer - and smile. But hold tight to what George Bernard Shaw said: "The fact that a true believer is happier than a skeptic is no more to the point than a drunk being happier than a sober person." The frenzy and fervor behind what the fanatic says does not hold water to a more even-keeled, scientific manner of understanding the mysteries of the human condition.

34. *A drunken state of mind.* Intoxication brought on by the fever of one's ideals is a dangerous combination. Angry-behaving people get themselves intoxicated in and by their efforts to control and command. Fueled by their own self-righteous emotions, eventually they often end up choking on their own vomit as the hangover from all the harm caused by their self-righteous indignation begins to set in - that is, their social group avoids them.

35. *Turning one's back on and making oneself allergic to preferences, wishes, wants, and desires that would allow for pursuing more constructive alternative possibilities.* Preferences extend possibilities; demands narrow-mindedly limit them. Humans have a knack for making themselves allergic to preferences. They are very quick to acknowledge something or a certain type of behavior as preferable and good, but rather than follow through with their projects and relationships with these wants, they are quick to

leap-frog from a preference to a demand; to go from making themselves preferably motivated to demandingly insistent, that is: "Because something or someone's behavior is good and desirable, it must exist; if it's good, I have to have it/experience it." This is the rallying cry of practically all humans and as a consequence of such demands a lot of anger is created - at self, toward others, or against the world.

36. *Magical thinking.* Anger is often presumed to be some sort of magical potion. The holder of this troublesome emotion surmises that someway, somehow, with all the energy created on anger's behalf and all this power invested thereof, change will be created. Anger reflects a razor's edge-type feeling that caters to omnipotence, blinding one from the truth: that the production of energized, godlike, magical thinking will bring about change - for the worse!

37. *Problem creation, not problem resolution.* Angry-acting people don't negotiate well, fail to test out new ideas, and avoid exercising compassion and tolerance. As a result, the angry solution creates more problems. Taking a bad situation and making it worse is a trademark of anger.

38. *Leading to a duplication of oppression.* True, anger can oppose oppression, but more often than not those oppressed will pick up the oppressor's aggressive ball and run with it. Angrily opposing oppression is often followed by the oppressor taking on the harsh mottoes of his or her former adversaries; for example, survivors of child abuse are more likely than not to become abusive themselves. The European settlers came to this country seeking escape from religious oppression. Upon arriving, they began to shove Christianity, among other things, down the throats of the Native Americans. One of the peculiar aspects of anger is that when thrown into the human relationship mix it practically always finds a way to use its mentality and expression to defeat emotional sanity.

39. *An emotion that is difficult, at best to channel constructively.* Most experts tell us, "It's not anger but what you
do with it that matters." Well, that is certainly one way to
look at it. Looking a little closer will reveal what humans
often do with anger: putting us a little closer to possible
nuclear and other warlike destruction. Far better to snuff
anger out before it gets in gear and takes on wildfire proportions. Channeling anger constructively leaves a risk
factor whose harmful consequences are difficult to over-
estimate.

40. *A paradox.* Acting out of control as a means of gaining
control is a contradiction in terms, yet that is what anger-
expressional addicts propose as an upside-down, ass-
backwards remedy to this overreactive problem.

41. *A show of inferiority, not superiority.* Angry-acting people
in the throes of their infantile antics expose feelings of inferiority; holier-than-thou-ism is the angry camouflaged
message, unworthier-than-all-ism is the content within the
statement. Angrily blaming others as inferior permits es-
caping from blaming oneself as being subhuman.

42. *Powerless, not powerful.* Angry behaviors reveal a desperate, frantic attempt to control for deficiencies in power that
those who use force to prove themselves absolutely believe
they must have. If contrary-acting people were more at
peace with themselves, they wouldn't be taking such a warlike stance.

43. *Unhealthy and justified; the former if your goal is to live
more emotionally sound, the latter if your goal is to be
miserable.* Anger is unhealthy because of its harmful outcomes, though it is a normal feeling state created by most
people some of the time. It's just that being normal and in
the majority when it comes to expounding upon childlike
demands is not healthy, because they do not contribute to
one's long-range happiness and survival.

44. *Easier to restrain from it rather than express it - in the long
run.* In the short run, anger is a convenience item; it often

seems more convenient to vent its blastings. However, looking back on the aftermath of such emotional explosions, it can be plainly seen that due to the debris created from leveling almost everything and everyone in anger's sight, as difficult to restrain as it is, it is even more difficult not to restrain anger due to the nightmares and comedy of errors that trail anger's bombardments.

45. *A poor way to express a message.* Content of expression is lost in the sea of embitterment. Others will likely spook themselves by your "going off" in anger, running in the other direction to escape your wrath. In their hurry to leave, they will miss out on what you have to say.

46. *A separate, autonomous, distinct emotion that can be sorted out from annoyance, irritation, and displeasure.* The latter three feeling states contain preferences; anger is a result of demands, for example: "Because I *prefer* kinder, gentler treatment, you *must* (I *demand*) that you forever and always provide me with such." Anger can be identified, sorted out from other emotions, and changed by studying its philosophical premises, mainly carving out the distinction between desire, which is healthy, and demand, which is unhealthy.

47. *A poor method of persuasion.* Overpower people by pushing them against the wall and they may, temporarily at least, pretend to agree with your noble values. But the minute you leave, they are likely to (a) go back to what they believed to be their original correctness, and (b) avoid you in the future. Trying to ram your ideas down others' throats will leave you without an audience to teach due to your iron-handed, knuckle-sandwich methods of enticement.

48. *A self-defeating right of expression.* Due to free will and human limitations, individuals have rights to be angry and to be wrong. The trick is to not die with your rights on by exercising your unalienable rights only as they contribute to your long-range best interest. Anger is hardly in that helpful, make-life-run-smoother category.

49. *A clumsy, awkward, inefficient way of disinhibiting your-self.* Anger gets in its own way and the result is often a bad situation made worse. It's hard to walk and think straight if you can't see straight. Anger results in a lopsided approach to more clearly expressing understanding and resolving problems and concerns.

50. *The human thing to do, yet inhumane.* It is near impossible to hurt someone else without hurting yourself. The nature of anger is to encourage the mutual destruction of anger's participants. Therefore, though felt by practically all humans, it is against humans, and therefore inhumane.

51. *A poor way to stand up for yourself.* When angrily standing behind your convictions, you will likely arouse dander in others who will then oppose you all the more. Silence, agreement, understanding, and acceptance are harder to refute than anger.

52. *A preexisting tendency.* Being biological creatures first, some humans are simply more inclined to demonstrate a short fuse. These folks will be required to work extra long and hard to control their genetic tendency to destructively light their own emotional fire. Humans are temper-prone by nature rather than by nurture. To admit to these impulsive inclinations and to work hard, probably for the rest of one's life, to control them is the recommended task.

53. *Distortion.* Angry-acting people view the world through perverted eyes. Insistences drown out reason and logic, and, as a result, the world and people in it are viewed in ways that are figments of one's angry imagination.

54. *Lethal.* There is nothing you can do with anger that you can't do without it - except kill someone!

55. *Having characteristics of escalation.* Not only does anger feed upon itself but its expression is an anger enhancer; an invitation for others to act angrily also.

56. *Self-punishment for the negative actions of others.* It's difficult to do harm to others without doing harm to yourself. While you are angry, the other person may well be out

having the time of his or her life - while you sit home and angrily and sulkingly have none.

57. *"Two-year-oldism."* A stomping of one's feet, a moan here, and a groan there tips off anger as an infantile expression of protesting about gaining what one's little heart desires.

58. *Self-righteousness.* Proclaiming one's values as superior if not almighty is one of the intricacies of anger's anatomy.

59. *Sacredizing inconveniences.* Demanding to be the one - and only one - person in the universe to never be inconvenienced is a component of anger development.

60. *An agent of control.* Anger's expression attempts to force the issue of agreement, approval, and understanding by acting as an agent attempting to control for such niceties.

61. *Often having secondary problems of guilt, shame, low frustration tolerance, and self-depreciation.* Upon having observed themselves acting cuckoo, pitiful angry specimens are likely to give themselves a double whammy by telling themselves such intolerant, self-berating ideas as: "What a bad person I am for acting badly," "I can't stand feeling so upset," "How terrible it is that those who bore witness to me flipping my wig may no longer like me," and "What a varmint and venom I am for my despicable conduct."

This book will incorporate these 61 and other redefinitions of anger into its contents, all in an effort to:

- identify anger's anatomy.
- explore what can be done to dissolve anger's mechanics.
- more fully appreciate the advantages of dismantling its components.

In short, to do anger's dangers in before you get yourself done in by them.

Note. From *You Can Control Your Anger! 21 Ways To Do It* by Bill Borcherdt. Copyright © 2000, Professional Resource Exchange, Inc., P.O. Box 15560, Sarasota, FL 34277-1560.

Chapter 1 Review Questions

1. Which of the 61 dimensions of anger do you think is most dominant in self and others?

2. What is meant by anger as being an agent of control?

3. What is meant by anger as an addiction?

4. Why is anger a sign of emotional weakness?

5. Why is anger a poor problem-solving method?

CHAPTER 2

Misinformation about Anger - Critique and Corrections: Myths, Misconceptions, and Methods of Change

The purpose of this chapter is to identify and attack mistaken ideas about anger and discover sounder, more provable, and more helpful notions that provide a structure for constructive change that is practical and workable. Until a foundation of understanding on a topic is built upon solid, scientific ideas, good intentions will be sabotaged by poor, unverified methods. Part I will focus on discarding the bad myths and misconceptions about anger while Part II will clasp the good, substantiated, helpful tactics of constructively confronting this prevalent problem. Each stated myth or irrational belief (IB) about anger will be followed by a rational rebuttal (RR) that will provide ideas for challenging each misconception in the service of your emotional well-being.

Part I: Myths and Misconceptions

IB 1:   *"Anger is externally caused."*
RR: This preposterous, magical-thinking theory maintains that someone else's words and/or deeds or other un-

pleasant conditions of life wiggles/squirms/creeps into your gut and transplants anger. Given close thought, the emotional transplant theory is hilarious - so hilarious, in fact, that you would think that no one in his or her right mind would believe this voodooistic notion. Yet practically everyone who has ever walked this green earth believes and continues to hang on to this primitive idea. Such a belief puts you at the mercy of external circumstances, makes you the plaything of others, and leaves you on the edge of danger in coping with adversity. Anger is not caused by external events but by demanding that these outside-of-self happenings cease to exist.

IB 2:   "*Expression of anger gets rid of anger.*"

RR: Anger release has an amplifying rather than a diminishing effect. The more you curse frustration and the more you express anger, the *angrier* you become. Practicing expressing your anger will cause more anger because who and what you anger yourself at will likely not change (unless it's for the worse), regardless of how far you put your angry foot forward. The more anger production you manufacture, the better producer and manufacturer of anger you are likely to make yourself. In no time flat you will become well oiled and well versed at disadvantaging yourself in varying ways via your anger expression efforts; for example, abandonment by your social group, loss of health, and strain at work and in your relationships with your loved ones.

IB 3:   "*The angrier you are, the stronger you are.*"

RR: Bursting at the seams with anger makes for a pathetic sight. Angry bombshells reflect fear, insecurity, impotence, hurt, and emotional dependency. People in the heat of anger are psychological wimps. If they possessed self-assuredness, they would have little desire to defend themselves nor to take on such an exaggerated view of what they think others can do to them, that is, demean, discredit, or disgrace them, or put them down. Self-confidence would assist them in producing less angry emotional toil toward others and toward life circumstances that frustrate and deprive.

IB 4: "*Unless you get yourself angry and display its dramatic proportions, you will allow yourself to get walked on as a patsy.*"

RR: There are many ways to protect yourself and create a distance from others who act in displeasing ways other than licking your chops and fighting anger's fire with fire. Making yourself out to be a Doris or Donny doormat need not be the end result of (unangrily) standing up for yourself. Telling others how you feel without telling them off is an option to avoid angrily confronting others' meanness.

IB 5: "*What you see in the midst of anger is what you get.*"

RR: Appearances can be misleading. With anger:

What appears is:	*What you get is:*
Superiority	Inferiority
Invulnerability	Vulnerability
Power	Powerlessness
Strength	Weakness
Anger	Hurt
Fearlessness	Fearfulness
Independence	Dependence
Self-sufficiency	Self-deficiency
Self-confidence	Insecurity

IB 6:   "*If you don't get angry at yourself for getting yourself angry, you won't be motivated to correct your error in the future.*"

RR: On the contrary, compassion begins at home. The better able you are to forgive yourself, the more generous you are likely to be in forgiving others for their trespasses and the less angry you are likely to make yourself. "Scold the act but not the actor" is the counter to this erroneous idea.

IB 7:   "*Anger is healthy and justified.*"

RR: Anyone who thinks anger is healthy is asking for trouble and probably looking for an excuse to pop off so as to ventilate and to indulge in their angry addiction. Anger is justified if your goal in life is to make yourself miserable, to disadvantage yourself, and to walk around as if you had a ramrod shoved up your behind for the rest of your days.

IB 8:   "*Anger can constitute moral behavior under some circumstances.*"

RR: Anger is an immoral emotion because it is against humans and is a damnation of another human.

IB 9:   "*It's so easy to get oneself angry.*"

RR: In the very short run, maybe; in the long run, no. The frequent aggressive behavioral fallout from anger increases life's difficulties and problems, making anger harder on oneself when taking on a view of and a vision for the future. Anger's aftereffects are hard, not easy, to stomach.

IB 10:   "*Anger is a good way to communicate or express a message or your feelings.*"

RR: When you address others in anger, they will likely hear your drama while missing out on your content. This is because anger is an awkward, clumsy, inefficient means of getting your point across. Anger may induce others to stand at attention, but very little retention is likely to follow.

IB 11: *"Anger can solve certain problems."*

RR: Because of its divisive, inciteful nature, anger is a problem, not a solution. It serves as a wrecking crew for relationship and practical opportunities. As it builds up a head of steam, anger gets uncooperative, compromising results.

IB 12: *"If you don't express anger it will backfire on you."*

RR: Anger will backfire on you if you do express it, because each time you give vent to this hideous emotion you rehearse and strengthen anger as a symptom.

IB 13: *"Anger has to be either expressed or suppressed, repressed, stockpiled, or swept under the rug."*

RR: This absolute, this-way-or-that line of (un)reasoning leaves out what Rational Emotive Behavior Therapy (REBT) principles are famous for doing: dissolving anger. This is done by challenging and changing the demanding thoughts that created the anger to begin with.

IB 14: *"Because anger feels good it is good for you."*

RR: Anger and its immediate expression causes you to feel better but get worse. With practice, anger is made into being an automatic, repetitive response to your misgivings; your emotional and behavioral responses are gradually made into being less and less civilized.

IB 15: *"High and lengthy frustration about someone/something inevitably leads to and causes anger."*

RR: An individual can have high frustration and low-level or no disturbance (anger) or low frustration and high-level disturbance, largely depending upon how seriously the individual takes the seeming never-ending stressor. Humans do not respond the same to the same frustration.

IB 16:   *"Anger, displeasure, irritation, and annoyance differ in degree rather than in kind."*

RR: To understand REBT's anatomy of anger (and what you can do to dismantle it), it is helpful to understand the mechanics of emotions. Anger is different in kind, *not* degree, from displeasure, irritation, and annoyance. To appreciate this distinctiveness is to lead the way to corralling anger. Healthy preferences such as "I want/prefer to do well," "I like it better/prefer that others understand and cooperate with me," and "I wish/prefer that this problem in living would not exist" will create healthy emotions such as displeasure, irritation, and annoyance. These are healthy emotions because they will prevent you from making yourself angry at yourself when you falter, hostile toward others when they goof, and bitter toward life when it does not cater to you. Consequently, this quieter threesome (displeasure, irritation, and annoyance) will be in your best interest.

OK so far - but:
Humans are allergic to preferences and are quick to blow them up into demands such as:

- "Because I prefer to do well, therefore I must!"
- "Due to the fact that I prefer more cooperation and understanding from others, they must do so."
- "Because I prefer that problems in living not exist, they must not."

These demands will create unhealthy emotions such as anger, rage, and fury that will defeat the purpose of happier living. The split second that you take the quantum leap from a preference - in the form of a wish, want, desire, or hope - to a demand - in the form of a must, should, got to, ought to, or supposed to - is the very moment that anger distinguishes itself from displeasure, irritation, and annoyance. Part of Albert Ellis's genius was that he demonstrated how a few words can make a major difference in determining emotional sanity as opposed to emotional disturbance. These words reflect desire rather than demand.

IB 17:   *"Anger will release unpleasant thoughts and take despicable things off your mind."*

RR: On the contrary, anger will cause you to overfocus on who or what you are angering yourself about, resulting in a lingering effect that will have you stewing and brooding about matters of concern, rather than doing something about them when possible or accepting them when not being able to change them.

IB 18:   *"Anger is a good, effective method of persuasion; it gets others to do what you want them to."*

RR: Well, yes and no - but mostly no. If you use anger to try to intimidate others so that they agree with and patronize you, they will likely pretend to go along with your demands, but as soon as you leave their presence they will return to their old ways - with added resentment. Anger as a persuasive method may convenience the other to "freeze" in your presence only to never throw out the hostile wrinkles that have now been created in the relationship.

IB 19:   *"Because I am entitled and have a right to be angry I must exercise that right at any and every opportunity to do so."*

RR: Don't croak with your rights on, rather exercise them only if they contribute to your long-range happiness and survival.

IB 20:   *"If one studies the topic of anger and diligently prepares oneself to give it up, one should become the pillar of unangry mental health."*

RR: Sometimes the best way to study psychology is to not study psychology. Some of the most well-studied people on the topic of emotional disturbance are the biggest offenders of overreaction. That's often why they entered the psychological field to begin with - to try to better attend to their own emotional problems!

IB 21:   *"Unless I get myself angry at and disgusted with myself, I cannot overcome my anger problem."*

RR: To berate yourself for having a problem is to increase its frequency. To accept yourself with it is to lessen its frequency. The more you accept you, the less angry you will be.

IB 22:   *"When I'm feeling anger, others should accommodate me and be angry themselves - and if they really cared about me they would."*

RR: It is not a breach of loyalty to not sign up for the misery-likes-company syndrome. The less serious others take you in stark contrast to how serious you are taking yourself, the more of a favor they are doing you. Good friends will not sell themselves out to your immature hecklings.

IB 23:   *"Because I'm working hard against my anger, those against whom I normally fight fire with fire have to work on their angry outbursts too; and if they really gave a damn about me they would."*

RR: No evidence exists that others are required to carry forth
with the same goals as you. Everyone is different and
will decide if and when they will begin their own personal mental health projects.

IB 24:   *"Others must assist me in working against my problem
of anger by saying only what I want to hear, doing only
what I want them to do, or otherwise walking on thin
ice in patronizing my values more often."*

RR: Others are not required to perfume your intolerance by
tiptoeing around you and by saying and doing only
things that meet with your approval. Doing your emotional self-control work for yourself rather than demanding that others do it for you makes it more likely that it
will get done.

IB 25:   *"My counselor should take the responsibility to pave
the way for my taking charge of my emotions. If he were
truly competent and gave a damn about me, he would."*

RR: Better that you ask what you can do for yourself in your
counseling than demand what your counselor/counsel-
ing "should" do for you. That way you put the responsibility for better regulating your anger where it belongs:
on yourself.

IB 26:   *"Anger is a good way to disinhibit and motivate myself."*

RR: Because of its pigeonhole qualities, anger ordinarily
turns out to be a very poor way to unleash yourself.
Due to its limitations in other alternatives, anger will
beat disagreements to death while ignoring other, more
compromising and cooperative possibilities. Its rigid
nature will motivate you to consider and do one thing
and one thing only. The usual end result of such limitations of alternatives is to continue to motivate yourself

to do the wrong thing rather than to explore other options.

IB 27:   *"It's normal to feel angry, being normal is good, so therefore it's good to feel anger."*

RR: The first part of this premise is accurate: most people will anger themselves when inconvenienced. But what most people will do about anger is often nothing to brag about and more likely than not has far from a redeeming social significance. Anger, though the often human thing to do, is also inhumane because it threatens to destroy anyone who stands in its disagreeing way.

IB 28:   *"Anger has more advantages than disadvantages."*

RR: Watching the evening news on television provides a lifelike perspective to anger's (dis)advantages. Asking yourself what sort of problem solver you usually are when angry will provide further insight into what side of the pro and con anger argument you fall on.

IB 29:   *"Anger is a good way to stand up for yourself."*

RR: Many things are harder to refute than anger - silence, humor, understanding, and acceptance, to name a few. Sometimes the best way to stand up for yourself is to take problems of concern sitting down. When you use anger to stand up for yourself it often incorporates notions that attempt to put others down. By using anger to defend yourself you are inviting others to anger themselves all the more - which is bad.

IB 30:   *"Don't get mad (angry), get even."*

RR: This silly suggestion is a page directly out of the angry book. Its mentality is the same angry song and dance as anger as bittersweet revenge. It is simply another way of restating anger's childish, intolerant philosophies.

IB 31:   *"Unless you get yourself profusely angry at someone who has wronged you or ignored your wishes, insult will be added to injury, leaving you with a psychological black eye."*

RR: Bad-mouth you, discriminate against you, boycott you, yes! Insult or demean you, no! Insult, discredit, and disgrace are only things you can do to yourself. The long and short of such a circumstance is that anger reflects a dire need for acceptance and approval from others. Get rid of the need and you get rid of the anger. There never was an insult or a psychological injury to begin with; to realize this is to not consider anger to defend yourself against a nonexistent opponent.

IB 32:   *"Anger is learned from angry-acting models."*

RR: Human temperament is learned - if the learner is teachable. Humans have preexisting tendencies toward anger and its foundation in low frustration tolerance and impatience. Over the years I have been impressed by the number of single parents who report to me that their offspring are of similar temperament vintage as the absentee parent, whom the child may never have met! Humans are accidents waiting to happen, and for better or for worse, it is difficult to stifle their potential, anger or otherwise.

IB 33:   *"To be without anger is to be without emotion."*

RR: Because you transcend anger does not mean human feelings are beyond you. On the contrary, as you lessen angry inclinations you are in a better position to exercise your option on more pleasant emotions that anger will get in the way of expressing, such as excitement, exhilaration, and enjoyment. The E in REBT means emotiveness, not emotionlessness.

IB 34:   *"Anger isn't bad; it's what you do with it that is bad."*

RR: Famous last words. Humans aren't skilled at redirecting anger. History has proven what the human species has done with anger - not very much that's good, I'm afraid. Anger is a lethal emotion that, while feeding upon itself, paints a distorted view of life. It is simply not the nature of anger to lead one into constructive activity. Our human condition may well be an endangered species until we realize and act upon the reality that anger presents major risk factors that are not worth tampering with.

IB 35:   *"There are certain things you can't do/accomplish unless you are angry."*

RR: Again, yes and no. True, it may be difficult to harm, maim, or kill someone without anger's explosiveness; however, beyond such crippling acts there is nothing constructive you can do with anger that you can't do without it.

IB 36:   *"Anger can liberate those in bondage because it opposes oppression."*

RR: The problem with using anger to overcome oppression is that those oppressed, once liberated, tend to take on the same dictatorial, tyrannical views of their former oppressors. Anger against oppression is often made to go beyond what is necessary to simply establish independence. Anger does not know boundaries. A way had best be found to teach those with nuclear capability how to keep anger at arm's length from expression - for any purpose. To teach others, as sadly many mental health professionals do, to "go with your anger, don't let it build up," is strange not wise advice indeed!

IB 37:   *"No one would ever want to feel and express anger at no time, in no place, and under no conditions."*

RR: Who wouldn't want to practically never feel and express anger? Alas, someone in his or her right mind, that's who!

Part II: Methods of Change

Rational Emotive Behavior Therapy (REBT) was the original multimodal psychotherapy. As such, it uses a number of cognitive (thinking), emotive (feeling), and behavioral (action) methods to challenge and chase anger and its miserable, destructive aftereffects. The following philosophies, tools, and techniques can be used to get and keep anger on the run, killing it before it threatens to kill you.

1. *Challenge anger's philosophical foundations with self-confrontive questions such as:*

   - "Why do others not have a right to unintentionally *or* intentionally betray my values?"
   - "How can it be proven that others don't have a right to be (repeatedly) wrong (and not learn from their mistakes) on top of it all?"
   - "Is it really a valid idea to think that others don't have a right to be different? (Especially since all people are infinitely different.)
   - "Would it be democratic for others to require others to abide by my wishes?"
   - "Why must others only do things that I approve of?"
   - "Are my values (come on now) really as superior as I Godly make them out to be?"
   - "Is it really that almighty important that others always (or ever) accept me and never (or ever) not judge me?"
   - "Is it truly catastrophic when others balk and interfere with what I consider to be my best interests?"

- "Do I want to do what's better for me, or find the best way to spite the other?"
- "When others are not treating me fairly, isn't that all the more reason to be fair to myself, and not fight fire with fire?"
- "Where is it written that others cannot trespass on my land full of values?"
- "Why should not others follow their own nose rather than mine?"
- "Do others have free will (which is it) or my will?"
- "Would it not be better for me to bend my thinking about that which I disagree with in others than to get myself bent out of shape regarding such distinctions?"

2. *Sidestep perfect rationality.* Just because you know something about the topic of rational thinking doesn't mean that you have to be a pillar of mental health. Leave room for accepting yourself with your fallible nature so that when you do inevitably slip in your efforts to control your emotions, you don't turn it into a major setback by putting yourself down for your error.

3. *Leave margin for error.* These four little words will allow you to approach your relationships with others in a more tolerant way. To know what to realistically expect of self and others is a central component of mental health - and of regulating anger.

4. *Intentionally hush your words.* Simply lowering your voice can contribute to greater emotional control, both within yourself and in others' response to you.

5. *Emphasize a philosophy of compassion.* Self-forgiveness for flying off the handle and other-forgiveness for similar stoogeful behavior promote concentrating on making fewer errors in the future.

6. *Will training.* Put your stubbornness to good use. Relentlessly refuse to get yourself angry. Dig in your heels and

determine, "I don't have to make myself angry about anything, nor put myself down when I do."

7. *Challenge what you believe is the absolute superiority of
your values.* Because your views are highlighted in your
own mind and therefore different from another's doesn't
mean that they are better.

8. *Learn to agree to disagree, to argue, but to do so constructively by avoiding:*

   • *Grave digging.* Arguing about the past will likely open
   up old, hostile wounds.
   • *Finger pointing.* Try to point to the problem to be resolved
   rather than blaming the other.
   • *Mind reading.* Check out your hunches as to whether
   someone is angry at you, lest you set in motion a chain of
   misunderstandings.
   • *Score keeping.* It takes a long time to find something that
   doesn't exist, like discovering who is more right and who
   is more wrong on a given issue.
   • *Hitting below the belt.* Avoid accusations, names, and
   insinuations that your associate typically angers himself
   or herself about. Such dirty-pool tactics contribute to
   anger escalation.

9. *Create a philosophy of unangry restraint.* Walk away from
trouble, but if it continues to follow you, restrain yourself
from fighting fire with fire. If you simply restrain yourself
from anger expression (which is preferable to not restraining yourself) but continue to damn the other person under
your breath, you will strengthen preexisting intolerant,
condemning philosophies about people whom you view as
being in the wrong.

10. *Practice telling others how you feel (when it's to your advantage to do so) without telling them off.* Responsible
self-expression such as this encourages all concerned to
be more responsible for themselves.

11. *Question conventional wisdom's theory that it is unhealthy to live without expressing much anger.* The horrors of restraint are grossly overplayed in that more problems come from *lack of* - not *due to* - restraint.
12. *Don't use anger as nerve gas in order to perfume feelings of guilt.* While refusing an unfair request, you aren't required to use anger to disinhibit yourself; in protecting yourself from a critical-acting person, it is not necessary that you blow your emotional stack prior to doing so.
13. *Don't use anger to camouflage hurt.* If you find that hurt precedes anger, admit that you are taking the matter personally and causing yourself hurt rather than coming on like angry gang-busters to deny hurt's existence. Hurt may not be as exciting or anti-boring as anger, but sometimes it can be a not-so-visible feeling state. First come, first serve - including the many instances that hurt arrives before anger is kicked into gear. Attend to hurt as self-blame and/or self-pity so that the correct emotional disturbance is attended to.
14. *Look at the part of the relationship that is fuller.* Help to dissolve angry inclinations by recalling and focusing upon pleasant experiences with, and strengths, advantages, and resources of, the person you are starting to get an angry bead on.
15. *Use rational-emotive imagery REBT style.* Clients are often quite surprised to discover that with this technique they are quite capable, often in the first session, to control both their primary-level anger (anger at another) and/or their secondary anger (anger at self for getting them self-angry). This can be done by an adjustment in their thinking or imagery portraits. The technique can be used at the primary level as follows:

   • Clients are asked to close their eyes and picture a real-life situation that they typically anger themselves in.

- Clients are then directed to purposely make themselves angry at the happenings in this scene; for example, cause themselves to cringe in their gut, to churn a good case for anger.
- Then, they are told to give the signal "now" when they are able to reach an angry pitch.
- Last, they are requested to continue to imagine the same scene in which they produced the anger, but this time to substitute a different, noninterfering emotion in place of anger, such as keen displeasure or decided annoyance; to switch gears by way of feeling states. They are then told to open their eyes once they are able to complete the full circle from uncivilized anger to civilized irritations.

The same tactic can be used at the secondary level: anger at oneself for getting oneself angry.

- Clients are asked to close their eyes and picture a circumstance in which they foolishly angered themselves.
- Clients are then instructed to put themselves down for their anger escapade so as to bring on a pervasive sense of guilt/shame.
- Then, they are instructed to say "now" when they are able to self-depreciate themselves en route to feeling guilty about their angry drama.
- Finally, they are asked to continue to imagine their angry explosion minus the self-blame and guilt; to instead bring on more functional emotions such as regret and remorse. They are told to open their eyes after successfully completing the cycle of emotional change.

16. *Learn to contain anger by not giving yourself low frustration tolerance about the facts of its existence:* that is, not "I can't stand feeling so angry," but "I can stand this feeling called anger, though I sure don't like it."

17. *Practice patronizing your adversary.* Neutralize your anger with hobnobbing strategies that allow you to act pleasantly and complimentary toward your opponents even if you don't feel like doing so. Killing with kindness is better than killing them bodily.

18. *Remove yourself.* Take a time out from the conflict or aggravation of the moment so as to refreshen your tolerance level.

19. *Avoid certain topics.* Refuse to discuss dead-end topics that history has shown will only egg on feuding and fighting.

20. *Arrange for tradeoffs.* Agree to do things for the other in exchange for him or her doing something for you. That way, rather than angrily doing things *to* each other, you will be more likely to unangrily do things *for* each other.

21. *Partake in constructive distractions.* Exercise, reading, listening to music, or mastering an activity you have not been skilled in are but a few examples of simple pleasures that can divert you from anger.

22. *Take on a philosophy of nonreciprocation.* Train yourself to give, help, assist, and provide to others with little or no expectation of a return - lest you tempt yourself to anger yourself for giving so much and gaining so little when your efforts are not acknowledged.

23. *Offer compromises.* Suggesting something in between your position and another's ideas can provide a softening effect for all concerned.

24. *Understand that most people are for themselves and their values rather than having nothing else better to do than be against you.* This insight can neutralize anger that is related to the defensive idea that others are out on a search-and-destroy mission toward you.

25. *List the advantages of restraint and the disadvantages of anger.* Using this list as a daily reminder can prevent anger rebuttals that frequently are made to escalate.

26. *Understand that it's <u>not</u> easy to get yourself angry.* Appreciate that the long-range difficulties of anger far outweigh the immediate conveniences of anger expression.

27. *Learn words that cue restraint,* such as "cool your jets," "lighten up," "chill out," "hold your horses," "it's not the end of the world," "stop and think (including about your thinking)," and "give yourself some slack."

28. *Ready yourself with prepared statements that are insulated from anger, such as:*

    - "I don't have to answer to you."
    - "I don't agree with you."
    - "I strongly disagree."
    - "I definitely don't think that is right."
    - "You, but not everyone is entitled to your opinion."
    - "It sounds like you have some strong feelings on this matter."

29. *Read rational literature about anger.* Some examples are: *Overcoming Frustration and Anger* by Paul Hauck; *How to Control Your Anger Before It Controls You* by Albert Ellis; or *Dealing With Anger Problems: Rational-Emotive Therapeutic Interventions* by Windy Dryden. Each of these books tracks and enlightens about anger with the REBT perspective. Study is ordinarily called for in mastering any new subject, and the important topic of anger is no exception.

30. *Post reminders of your anger problem in the form of signs* that read, "Others have a right to be wrong," "Others don't have to go by my book," "I am (not) the Lord God Almighty," "I don't run the universe yet," "I don't have to act like a 2-year-old," "I (don't) know what is best for everyone," and "Everyone is entitled to their (not my) opinion."

31. *Especially get rid of the hydraulic view of anger that says you must vent this powerful emotion or it will flow out in self-harming ways.*

32. *Seek honest feedback.* Ask someone who you can trust to be honest with you and see if they will track your less angry efforts and report what they see.
33. *Look at history.* Take 5 minutes and run through your mind the many problems anger has caused through the centuries. See if you can still honestly believe what many experts will tell and sell you: "It's not anger that's a problem, but what you do with it."
34. *Get yourself in touch with the self-righteous, elitist, bigoted, all-or-nothing thinking components of anger.*
35. *Stick to judging behaviors; avoid judging people.*
36. *Rebuke the sacredness from your values.*
37. *Motivate yourself by adopting a philosophy of challenge.* You can be one of the few people who can overcome the temptation to not give others "undamning acceptance" - thus evaporating your anger.
38. *Tape-record yourself when angry and play the tape back as a good <u>object</u> lesson in how to not win friends and influence people while making yourself miserable and acting miserably toward others.*
39. *Put prevention ahead of cure.* Do rehearsals in your own mind that will prepare you to act more democratically and civilized when tempting yourself to cook your own angry goose.
40. *Accept the fact that you will sometimes give yourself angry emotional transgressions, but try to keep them down to a roar in terms of their frequency, strength, and duration.* Be realistic with yourself by agreeing to try to work at feeling/ expressing anger less frequently, more minimally intensely, and for shorter periods of time.

Note. From *You Can Control Your Anger! 21 Ways To Do It* by Bill Borcherdt. Copyright © 2000, Professional Resource Exchange, Inc., P.O. Box 15560, Sarasota, FL 34277-1560.

Chapter 2 Review Questions

1. Why is it a myth that anger is externally caused?

2. Why and how are anger's appearances misleading?

3. What do you believe to be the most harmful irrational belief about anger, and why?

4. What do you think is the most effective rational rebuttal in countering anger?

5. What method for changing anger makes the most sense to you?

CHAPTER 3

The Three Faces of Anger:
Its Presence at Practically All Scenes of
Emotional Disturbance Crimes

The premises of this chapter are:

1. When individuals either break a promise to themselves, find that others have broken a promise to them, or discover that life has reneged on an alleged contract with them, and the individuals demand that they not betray their own values or that others and life not turn tail on them either, anger results.

2. The specific self-sentences that create anger are: "*I* have to/must be perfect (including controlling my anger)"; "It's horrendous and awful when I don't"; and "I'm bad for being badly out of line with my values." "*You* have to/must treat me well and good (especially if I treat you well and good)"; "It's horrible and terrible when you don't"; and "You're bad for badly trespassing on my sacred values." "*Life* has to/must do well by me in granting me all the things that I would otherwise miss"; "It's a catastrophic calamity when it doesn't (especially when I double up on my efforts to bust a gut to succeed at my goals and proj-

ects)"; and "Life is lousy for not providing me with the lousy breaks necessary for me to break through to my desires and ambitions."
3. Practically all of what is called emotional disturbance is really some form of anger. Its presence seemingly can be found no matter which way you turn: anger at self for one's problems and deficiencies, anger at others for their flounderings and falterings, and anger at life for all its loopholes and potholes, too numerous to mention.
4. This anger triangle and practically all that it contains can be dissolved. This resolution and dissolution of anger can be done via a combination of cognitive, emotive, and behavioral tactics.

Before reviewing how to think, feel, and behave differently to correct anger, I will discuss what not to do with anger that exists oh, so abundantly.

- *Don't suppress or repress your anger feelings.* Stockpiling your animosities and sweeping them under the rug usually can be made to last only so long. Besides, it takes a lot of energy to restrict your awareness with this pushing-out-of-mind method. Life is made to come to a screeching halt. More constructive personal goals are put on hold while excess energy is expended so as to keep a tight lip and tight lid on anger.
- *Don't express your angry, spiteful feelings.* Ventilating your despisements will only serve to strengthen them. A boomerang effect occurs as your anger goes out the back door, only to reenter through the front door due to your inability to change the tune that caused the anger to begin with, such as: "I must do well," "You must treat me well," or "Life must do well by me."
- *Preferably don't distract, divert, sublimate, or channel your intense feelings, even if done in a fully or semi-constructive manner,* such as weight lifting, reading for

lengthy periods of time, jogging for miles at a clip, or doing anything else in excess. Many otherwise constructive activities taken to an extreme and used for the wrong reasons - that is, to avoid taking a look at how the anger was self-created to begin with - are not constructive anymore. Do the right thing for the right reason. Engross yourself in your vital activities not simply to *feel* better by putting anger in a compartment and acting as if it isn't there, but also to *get* better by flushing out and challenging the core cause of your anger: the demanding ideas that you, others, and life "ought to" be different than they are. You can run from the fact(s) of your anger, but you can't hide from its structure. Better that you 'fess up than fight against examining its existence.

- *Don't use anger as a protest.* Emotional disturbance is a protest against reality; a stubborn, pig-headed refusal to accept what exists, that is, that you're not acting well or that others and life aren't treating you well. That protest ordinarily comes in the form of a "should," a "must," or a "have to." Such disclaimers often make matters worse because they put more pressure on all concerned, making it more likely that anger will break through. The refusal to accept what is as plain as the nose on your face often contributes to depression that is preceded by the hopelessness that stems from the reality that no matter how much you whine and scream, you still will be unlikely to be able to act or to get the universe and the people in it to conduct themselves more rationally!

- *Don't deny its existence.* A philosophy of admittance is a prerequisite to beginning to unshackle yourself from anger. Without ownership for your feelings, you will make yourself dependent upon others to change before you can feel better. When anger exists, it exists - and it is created by you.

- *Don't get yourself defensive.* There is no need to explain, lest you overexplain and eventually put yourself over a barrel with your struggle and frustration in getting others to understand the *seeming* reasons for your increase in anger production. You're human, and humans oftentimes make themselves foolishly and stupidly angry. Just remember you're not stupid nor a fool because of your negative manners. That recall in itself will produce compassion, which will likely reduce anger, because compassion ordinarily begins at home. Self-forgiveness makes easier other-forgiveness, which in turn reduces anger on all fronts.
- *Don't counterattack.* By all means, don't let yourself become other-directed in following the lead of another's upsets. This "get even" mentality can only lead to destruction of people, places, and things. A million and one wrongs do not make a right; besides, along the way you may find yourself dying with your rights to ugly rebuttal on.

As indicated, anger is a very comprehensive problem that is likely to be a major factor in practically all emotional and behavioral problems. To arrest its effects is to put all concerned at greater rest than risk. Observe others, monitor yourself, and see if all the emotional disturbance that you bear witness to is not a direct, visible result of one or more points of the anger triangle: one corner for anger at yourself, another for anger at others, and the third corner reserved for life and/or the world. If anger is such a dominant emotion, there is no way to go but up by better controlling, if not dissolving, it. This can be done by sampling the cognitive, emotive, and behavioral tools listed on the following pages.

1. ***Cognitive means of dissolving anger:***

    (a) *Disputing irrational ideas that cause anger.* Anger is philosophically based. It is caused not by frustrating life circumstances or by your inability to do what you preferably would like to do to change such displeasing matters but by your up-high-on-your-pedestal demands that frustration in life not exist and/or that you must be able to change that which you find deficient. Counter, dispute the specific self-sentences found in the second paragraph of this chapter with:

- "Where is the evidence that I have to/must be perfect (including controlling my anger), that it's horrendous and awful when I don't, or that I'm bad for being badly out of line with my values?"
- "How can it be proven that others must/have to treat me well and good (especially if I treat them well and good), that it's horrible and terrible when they don't, and that others are bad for badly trespassing on my not-so-sacred values?"
- "Where is it written that life has to/must do well by me in granting me, me, me, me, (infinite) all the things that I would otherwise miss, that it's a catastrophic calamity when it doesn't (especially when I double up on my efforts to bust a gut to succeed at my goals and projects), and that life is lousy for not providing me with the lousy breaks necessary for me to break through to my desires and ambitions?"

Answer to the three questions: "There is none" (no evidence), "it can't (be proven)," and "no place (is it written)." Upon forcefully and strongly convincing yourself of these three answers, it is likely that anger will be put on the back burner, if not dissolved or evaporated.

(b) *Repeatedly review the following A to Z anger control coping statements until they become second nature in your thinking.* Repetition is the mother of learning, and drilling yourself with these statements, each of which reflects a philosophy of tolerance and acceptance, can go a long way toward interrupting your tendency to trip your own trigger and be ever so quick to reload. Daily, several times a day if necessary, rivet these rational ideas designed to curtail anger, until you get to know some of them like your social security number or middle initial. See for yourself if you are not then better equipped to regulate your anger on all three fronts.

A. "Others have a right to be wrong."

B. "Others have free will - not my will."

C. "I can stand it when others act badly."

D. "I do not have a monopoly on truth. Best I not con myself into believing that I do."

E. "Others do not have to treat me fairly."

F. "Because I'm nice to others doesn't mean they have to be nice back."

G. "Don't take others as seriously "as they sometimes take themselves."

H. "Others aren't bad for acting badly."

I. "What I would like from others is my business; what they want to give me is their business."

J. "People have a right to betray and trespass on my values."

K. "Others can be as different from me as they choose."

L. "My values are not sacred."

M. "It's undemocratic to think others must honor and obey my wishes."

N. "It's not awful when others don't give me my piece of taffy."

O. "Disappointments are not disasters because of others' poor conduct."

P. "Others can purposefully and intentionally select against and disadvantage me!"

Q. "Fair, kind treatment is nice but not necessary."

R. "Because I'm not the General Manager of the Universe (yet), others are not required to abide by my wants or dictates."

S. "I don't have to have my own way."

T. "Fact: Others do not make me angry, I make myself angry about their undesirable behavior."

U. "Best I not act demandingly, condemningly, or punitively."

V. "Best I not blame others for their faults and shortcomings."

W. "The fact that I find others' conduct a hassle does not make it a horror."

X. "Baloney that thou shalt have no other values before mine."

Y. "Others have a right to not accept me and to judge me badly."

Z. "Best I avoid the 11th commandment that causes my anger: 'My will be done.' Otherwise, I'll continue to play God and fight like the devil."

(c) *Learn your ABCs of emotional self-control as invented by Albert Ellis, PhD, originator of Rational Emotive Behavior Therapy (REBT), as a method of applying the disputations and coping statements listed previously.*

Most models of human behavior emphasize the happenings of life in efforts to determine the origin of

THE ABC'S OF ANGER REEDUCATION

A	IB's (Irrational Beliefs about self, another, life that cause the anger)	C	D (Dispute, different way of thinking)	E (New Effects)
You, another, conditions of life betray your values.	IB₁ "I, others, life must be perfect, do well, do well by me."	Anger at self, another, or life for thwarting your ideals.	D₁ "Where is the evidence that I, others, life must do well, be perfect?"	E₁ Feel more at peace with self, others, life.
	IB₂ "It's terrible, awful, horrible when I, they, it doesn't do perfectly well."		D₂ "How can it be proven that it is AWFUL when I, others, life balks at my not-so-sacred values?"	E₂ Take on new, rational philosophies for future applications.
	IB₃ "I can't stand to do the wrong thing or have the wrong thing done to me."		D₃ "Where is it written that I can't tolerate or stand anything as long as I'm above ground?"	E₃ Act more constructively and civilly with social group and toward self.

IB₄ "I, others, life is bad for badly betraying what I think is absolutely correct."

D₄ "Is there documentation that I, others, or life are evil for blockading my values?"

D₅ "I have a right to be wrong."

D₆ "Others have a right to be wrong."

D₇ "Life does not have to grant me the things that I miss nor eternal bliss."

anger. That perspective loses the individual's control factor: the thinking that actually created the anger, leaving the individual at the mercy of his or her, others, and life's flaws and deficiencies. Track down your thinking at "B," and ask yourself "Where does this thinking get me?" and "What would be a better way to think for me to get better emotional results?" Avoid such false ideas as:

- "That got me mad."
- "He pissed me off."
- "I became upset."
- "It makes me mad."
- "That got under my skin."
- "Such things trip my trigger."
- "I got angry."

Sit yourself down, outline the ABC model, and use it as a mechanism of discovering:

- What is happening at "A."
- What you are thinking/telling yourself at "B."
- What feeling do you experience at "C" as a result of your self-statements at "B."
- What would be a different way to think, to debate, and dispute at "D" your original beliefs.
- What new effects at "E" you sense from looking differently, more tolerantly, acceptingly, and forgivingly at "D." Take a long, hard look at the fact that just as you are an active participant in creating your own anger at self, others, and life, you can likewise be an active participant in dissolving it by addressing and changing your ideas that caused it to begin with.

(d) *Take your learnings to a higher level by explaining to others the ABC model of emotional self-control.* As you teach others the anatomy of anger and what can be done to combat its development, you may relearn at a clearer level what it is you wish to apply. One of the best ways to learn something is to teach it to others.

(e) *Do a rational debate.* Track irrational ideas and their counters by formally debating with yourself using the following formula: On the left side of a blank piece of paper, list all the irrational ideas you can think of that are at the root of your anger. On the right side, list their rational counters - notions that are provable and help you to feel more the way you want to feel and less the way you don't want to feel. Then, proceed to debate with yourself, arguing about and uprooting yourself of the ideas that cause your anger. For good measure, put the personal debate on tape and play it back and/or debate in front of a mirror where you can figure the expressive, emotive factor into how solidly you are building a case for emotional containment. The written debate would look like this:

IRRATIONAL IDEALS	RATIONAL COUNTERS
1. "I need to succeed."	"It would be terrific to succeed but not life threatening if I didn't."
2. "Others must understand me and treat me well."	"Relationships run smoother when I'm understood and treated well, but I don't require understanding or to be treated well."
3. "Getting what I want from my life projects must be made easier, and it is simply tragic when it isn't."	"I like it when matters of life come more naturally and easily, but it's hardly awful when they don't."

IRRATIONAL IDEALS *(Cont'd)*	RATIONAL COUNTERS *(Cont'd)*
4. "People don't have a right to be wrong, especially intentionally, purposefully, and willfully so."	"People do have a right to be wrong, including being especially, intentionally, and willfully so."
5. "Others should listen to me!"	"I like it when others value my opinion; thankfully my life doesn't depend upon their doing so."
6. "What a bad person he is for treating me badly."	"If he is bad for acting badly, then all humans would be bad for doing so, and this is hardly correct - people behave both well and badly, but they are not good for doing the right thing nor bad for doing the wrong thing."

(f) *Time projection.* Think of how much less significant what you are presently angering yourself about will be in the future. Giving yourself the opportunity to sense how much your anger will likely fizzle out in the future can encourage a lessening of stress in the present. Many angry episodes are soon forgotten, and this extension into time permits you to better appreciate that hopeful possibility.

(g) *Attribution.* Attributing and explaining to yourself what another's contrary behavior tells you about them and their emotional problems, rather than giving yourself emotional problems about their harsh conduct, prevents you from defining yourself by and making yourself miserable about another's harshness.

2. ***Emotive means of dissolving anger:**whatever*

(a) *Learn the principles of undamning acceptance when addressing human error, and unconditional self-acceptance (USA) when sizing up your blunders.*

Much emotional relief can be gained from passing judgment on the behavior of self and others without defining individuals by their wrongdoing. Ideas that reflect philosophies of undamning acceptance and unconditional self-acceptance include:

- "Condemn the sin but not the sinner."
- "Judge behaviors, not people."
- "Protect yourself, but don't retaliate."
- "Reprimand behaviors but not people."
- "Rate actions but not people."
- "People are not bad for acting badly."
- "Stupid behavior may be performed by a non-stupid person."
- "Foolish behavior may be performed by a non-fool."
- "Get after the misconduct, but don't get after the person."
- "Hold yourself and others accountable for misdeeds without condemning yourself or them for making them."

(b) *Practice rational-emotive imagery.* Practice doesn't make perfect, but it sure can help, including practicing dissolving your anger. Such rehearsal sessions won't automatically assure a less angry state of mind, but it is unlikely that you will learn how to keep a lid on your overreactions and personalizations without it. This imagery exercise is a mechanism of practicing dissolving anger toward others. First, close your eyes and vividly picture the person whom you make yourself angry at for doing what comes natural for him or her - rocking the boat of your values, perhaps even intentionally so. Then, literally make yourself angry and knotted up in your gut about this matter of seeming all-important betrayal. Last, clearly picture the same scene, only this time cause yourself to lighten up a little rather than tighten up a lot, and substitute an emotion that is something less than anger - perhaps disappointment, annoyance, or displeasure. See if, by thinking more tolerantly and acceptingly, you can make this emotional switch. I find that a large majority of clients are able to do so and, with practice, are able to make themselves angry less often, with diminished intensity, and for shorter periods of time.

(c) *Practice empathy training.* Listen to the who and not the what. Make an effort to understand and accept the other person's anger, rather than get yourself caught in it. Do this by reflecting back to the other the feelings you sense he or she has about the matter of concern. Such active understanding of another's feelings helps to neutralize them, and the angry wind is likely to be taken out of the other's angry sails. It's simply difficult to jawbone with someone who has the skill and takes the time to understand you at the feeling level. Examples of empathic understanding include:

- "It sounds like you have some strong feelings about the matter."
- "It sounds like you have thought long and hard about the views that you seem to feel so strongly about."
- "I sense you feel angry about the matter."
- "It's no fun to be treated unfairly, is it?"
- "It's difficult to manage feelings when they're so strong, isn't it?"
- "I sense that this wasn't exactly what you expected, to say the least."

(d) *Identify positive experiences that you have had with the other person and the pleasant feelings associated with such encounters.* Escalate, blow up these pleasantries; otherwise, you will likely remain angry and miss out on a fuller appreciation of the other.

(e) *Try to gauge your conduct toward others' mistakes with the guiding light of these four little words: "Leave margin for error."* Accepting the remarkably fallible nature of the human condition can help to diminish otherwise hostile feelings. Knowing and accepting what to realistically expect from another human being can dissolve much anger.

(f) *Purposefully antiexaggerate.* Make it a point to see others' ill-advised behavior as a part of life rather than bigger than life. Minimizing descriptors such as "terrible, awful, horrible, totally uncalled for" can help you to better keep angry feelings under wraps.

(g) *Minimize emotional dependency.* By seeing that you don't NEED others' understanding, cooperation, approval, appreciation, and so on, you can emotively nip in the bud anger that erupts when someone doesn't deliver what had been defined by you as a lifeline requirement. The more emotionally sufficient you make yourself, the less anger you will create.

(h) *Keep your preferences; let go of your demands.* Defining your preferences, desires, goals, values, and ambitions will arouse healthy feelings of anticipation, eagerness, and hopes; insisting upon such desires will result in feelings of anxiety, worry, and fear. Feelings can be controlled by hanging on to your dreams and schemes while not attaching life or death meaning to them.

(i) *Monitor pet demanding and exaggerating self-statements that trigger anger and try to minimize them in your vocabulary.* These might include:

- "She has no right to treat me this way."
- "Who does he think he is?"
- "She should know by now that I feel angry when she acts that way."
- "She makes me mad."
- "He really gets to me."
- "She likes to always make me mad."
- "I'll give him a dose of his own medicine."
- "No one should have to put up with this."
- "He has to respect my wishes."
- "She oughta have her head examined."
- "What a clod he is for acting badly."
- "She should have learned her lesson by now."

(j) *Use prepared messages/statements.* Preparing yourself for the heat lest you get yourself overheated can be helpful for the purpose of keeping your angry shirt on. These include:

- "That's only your opinion."
- "No matter what you say, I still have value to myself."
- "Your opinions are your cup of tea, not my poison."
- "What do you think your harsh criticism of me tells about you?"
- "It sounds like you identify yourself as an expert on the subject."
- "Now we have heard part of the story."
- "Is there anything else that you have to say on the matter?"

- "You're entitled to your opinion, and I don't have to get myself angry about it."

(k) *Find some agreement/truth to the other's negative barbs.* By agreeing at least in part and/or by earmarking the truth that is practically always there, a different emotive tone within yourself and between you and the quick-on-the-negative-trigger other can be created. Possible partially agreeing statements include:

  - "I never looked at it quite that way."
  - "Why didn't I think of that."
  - "Sometimes I do err in the ways you're pointing out."
  - "Not many people would take the time to examine the ins and outs of this matter as detailed as you have."
  - "I can understand how you can conclude what you have."
  - "You are correct here; there are some shades of gray to consider."

(l) *Lower your voice when expressing strong feelings.* This simple act alone can buffer angry feelings.

(m) *Bask in the feelings of accomplishment that relate to unangry restraint.* Consider how good you will feel in the aftermath of dissolving your anger. Going from "I have met the enemy, and the enemy is me" to "I have overcome the enemy" can be a very emotionally satisfying experience.

(n) *Passionately pursue a philosophy of challenge.* Such intent can invigorate and activate the emotional energy required to resist going for the angry bait. Forcefully call to mind that you can challenge yourself to be one of the few people who can overcome their short-fused inclination.

3. **_Behavioral methods of dissolving anger:_**

    (a) *Agree to disagree - but not too strongly or ruthlessly.* Point to your differences, but not in a way that tries to forcefully force-feed your values down the other's throat. Sidestep tendencies to say things that you know others will overreact to. Don't throw up past instances of disagreement that will throw gasoline on present differences. Don't try to impress on yourself and others that you are the good guy and others with distant views are the bad guys. Don't keep track of who has been right more often, and don't infer what the other's position is without checking out to see whether or not your assumptions are accurate.

    (b) *Periodically patronize the other.* Extending yourself to above and beyond the call of duty by being pleasant to another even when you don't feel like it, or saying pleasant things about someone you often feel anger toward (especially when the other can overhear you doing so) are behavioral moves that can help stem the tide of anger.

    (c) *Tell others how you feel - without telling them off.* Letting others know of your frustrations related to them without condemning them as human beings can assist in keeping your emotions within more civilized boundaries.

    (d) *Take on a philosophy of nonavoidance.* Repeatedly court circumstances in which you tend to push your angry buttons. Reclaim your will to restrain by exposing yourself to circumstances in which you have up until now semiautomatically angered yourself, but do so with a perspective that allows you to put your foot on the brake rather than on the gas pedal of your anger.

(e) *Set yourself up to be hassled.* Give your detractors material to work with by saying and doing things that are unpopular with them and for which they will likely become highly critical of and discriminatory toward you; for example, voice your support of abortion knowing your social group will likely select against you for it.

(f) *Do; don't stew.* Stay active. Pump your energy into constructive projects and mastery assignments. Such constructive distractions will at least temporarily divert you from feeling angry. Caution: Don't just *feel* better by keeping busy, but also *get* better by changing your demanding, anger-producing philosophies.

(g) *Don't offer unsolicited advice to people you are in disagreement with.* Advice given but not requested not only falls on deaf ears but tends to stoke up the flames of animosity. First, the advice is likely to go unappreciated and unheeded, leaving the sender to create ingratitude. Second, most people don't like to be told what to do, leaving the receiver to resent others' free-will, advice-giving offering.

(h) *Full-fledgedly physically remove yourself.* Rather than stick around and debate the issue, make a beeline for the nearest exit so as to shun argument and anger.

(i) *Adopt a philosophy of enlightened self-interest.* Putting yourself first and others a close second will make it easier to escape from the resentment that often is made to flow from attempts to do things for others that would be more advisable for them to do for themselves.

(j) *Adopt a philosophy of assertive effort.* By striving
     for what you want, you might discover not only that
     persistence against odds often can pay off, but also
     that such vital absorptions reduce anger, replacing
     it with feelings of accomplishment.

Face the three faces of anger - anger at self, others, and/or
life - by doing the following:

• Admit to the problem itself.
• Don't put yourself down for creating this unhealthy emotion.
• Track anger down to the demanding beliefs that caused
  the anger: that anger is self-created by faulty ideas and
  philosophies; that it is not externally caused; and that
  no one in the history of the human race has ever pissed
  anyone off.
• Give up the magical thinking where you lead yourself to
  believe that someone or something mystically transplants
  angry feelings into you.
• Change your irrational ideas that come under the um-
  brellas of demandingness, exaggerations, and self- and/
  or other-judgments.
• Behaviorally act upon your new way of thinking by
  making it a point to extend yourself in more pleasant,
  tolerant, and accepting ways that would contradict your
  emotionally fit-to-be-tied inclinations.
• Continue with the preceding efforts even if they feel
  unnatural and out of character at first. Making yourself
  feel unangry while going through life in more rational
  ways, like any experience that seems so different, ordinarily takes some getting used to.

Consumers of anger-control services are frequently given
two restrictive choices: Express anger or repress/suppress it.

Letting it all hang out at the one extreme and stockpiling anger or sweeping it under the rug at the other extreme are both ineffective and harmful coping mechanisms. A third alternative, which this book is devoted to addressing, is to healthfully dissolve anger via changing the philosophies that created it. By digesting and using the principles of Rational Emotive Behavior Therapy identified in this chapter, it is unlikely that anger's near ever-presence at the scene of emotionally disturbed crimes will be squelched to the realm of "never presence," but it will likely result in "less presence," with fewer emotionally disturbed crimes being committed as a result of anger.

Note. From *You Can Control Your Anger! 21 Ways To Do It* by Bill Borcherdt. Copyright © 2000, Professional Resource Exchange, Inc., P.O. Box 15560, Sarasota, FL 34277-1560.

Chapter 3 Review Questions

1. What are the two main choices given to consumers who wish to control their anger, and why are these options restrictive?

2. Do you agree that practically all emotional disturbance is some form of anger? Why or why not?

3. What is one thing that you think would be especially advisable not to do in controlling anger?

4. How and why can anger be considered to be a protest against reality?

5. What do you believe to be the most helpful of the A to Z anger control coping statements?

CHAPTER 4

Anger: Lots of Fire
Without Too Much Light -
Putting a Little Light on the Subject

Lights! Camera! Action! And so it goes with the human drama. The problem begins when anger is added to the equation. Anger produces action - but so does a bull in a china shop. Anger throws little light on the topic at hand, because discussants are likely to be too busy defending themselves and attacking one another. Little is disclosed with a camera, because participants ordinarily take distorted pictures when under the influence of anger; all the pictures they snap turn out red. This chapter is an effort to build a case for dissolving anger so as to permit participants to (a) take more constructive action about matters of concern, (b) shed more light on the facts of the discussion, and (c) take pictures that reflect reality while under the influence of logic and reason. Use of logic and reason so as to better service one's emotions, notably anger, underlies the premises of this book.

It is difficult to see the factual light of day due to anger's smoke screen. Using the principles of rational thinking, you can get through the emotional fog and bonfires of anger, so as to douse rather than fan its flames. A major error in sizing up your anger is that it throws more light on a topic; therefore, others will more closely listen to you when emotionally fired up under its influence. In truth, the more angry drama you use to support your case, the more attention will be paid to your whining and screaming, to the neglect of your accompanying message. Disadvantages of trying to communicate sense while in the wrap of anger's nonsense include:

1. *Audiences are more likely to listen - but less likely to hear.* When you are angrily expressing yourself, the medium is the message; the process becomes content. Though others may become more alert, they are likely to be attentive not so much to what you say but to the angry, 2-year-old manner that you use to deliver your information. Putting people in front of a verbal firing squad is not the best way to get them to understand you. They are likely to be too busy trying to think of lifesaving measures to hear what you have to say. Drama majors often get noticed by their audience - but to the neglect of their message.
2. *Interferes with brainstorming.* The anger-feeling person believes that he or she is 100% right and the other person is 100% wrong. This all-or-nothing mentality prevents the production of new ideas, without which problem solving will likely come to a screeching halt. Between social group members, brainstorming occurs when two or more people put their heads together and, in a nonjudgmental way, attempt to discover as many potential solutions to a problem that they can. Because of its one-sided nature - that is, "my way," "the way," - anger will block such efforts at problem-solving versatility and well-roundedness.
3. *Results in trying to do others in, rather than doing something about the problem.* Due to its damnation of another anatomy, anger makes it difficult, if not near impossible, to go from fighting each other on opposite sides of the table to fighting the problem on the same side of the table.

4. *Stifles creativity.* It is difficult for creativity to flourish in a climate of sameness. Yet, this is precisely the type of thinking that anger-feeling people try to create - that there are only two ways to look at things: the wrong way and their way. Anger prevents the deck of ideas from being shuffled in that there is only one card rather than the regular 52 (or more) to be shuffled and dealt; angry people just happen to know which one that is - and it just happens to belong to them! Others are discouraged from restructuring their thinking for fear that what is discovered will violate angry-feeling people's self-anointed values and standards. "No can do" is the attitude maintained by closed minded, anger-dominated people. Their way is their claim to fame, and they will be dipped if they will give others' ideas an opportunity to be tested.

5. *Conveys "holier than thouism."* Believing that your ideas are all right and that others are all wet disadvantages if not disables the opportunity to learn from people who think differently. "This is my way; what is your way?" is replaced with "This is THE way." As a result, no other ways are explored.

6. *Begets anger in others.* Open anger expression is an open invitation to match your fire with more fire. Carried to its extreme you have a holocaust, with eyes for eyes and teeth for teeth resulting in - guess what? A lot of blind, toothless people walking around, scratching their heads and licking their wounds wondering how such destruction could have happened to them. More rational communication is forced to wait and be tried another day.

7. *Often results in worry and anxiety.* Another emotion is frequently made to enter the scene: the fear felt by both the sender and the receiver that, if the outburst is not moderated, it will get out of hand. This wildfire concern has much basis in reality when one considers the vast amount of wanton destruction brought on by anger. Anger wrapped

in worry, fear, and anxiety makes for herky-jerky communication patterns at best.

8. *Distorts the truth.* Angry people enter their viewpoint with tunnel vision and pigeonhole thinking. Consequently, they don't see things as they are, but as they themselves, as angry-acting people, are. Anger as an overdone response to criticism, injustice, betrayal, and so on blocks a broader consideration of alternatives, some of which would come under the umbrella of the truth. The last thing angry-feeling people want to hear is a viewpoint that contrasts theirs; they want your views to respond to the rightness, facts, and truth - as they and they alone see it.

9. *Encourages slippery, sloppy, rigid thinking.* When the emotionally healthy notion that "You don't have to do well by me" is made to slip and slide into "but you really must," rigid thinking becomes entrenched, with anger being a consequence of such a slide. William Shakespeare said, "The whole world well knows, but nobody knows well." Most well know that others are not on this planet to convenience our values, but often, when it comes down to it, many don't know well and slip into a "but they really are" mode.

10. *Dashes hope.* Whatever or whomever the angry-acting person is hooting and howling at is unlikely to change - unless the change is for the worse! Defensiveness, denial, excuse making, and counterattacks are the far more likely discouraging responses to be experienced from others when you angrily try to shed some light on a matter of mutual concern.

11. *Feeds into magical thinking.* Screaming to the high heavens is often followed by the illusion that because of all the energy projected into your disenchantment, somehow, some way, things will change. Fire does not magically lead to light; extra helpings of drama are far more likely to lead to added misunderstandings than not.

12. *Disrespects individual differences.* "One size (and it just happens to be my size) fits all" overlooks the reality that there is more than one way to view the same scheme and that each human comes to his or her life circumstance with a different set of peepers and a different variety of values. Angry-acting people have a dickens of a time considering the possibility that others often sum life up (much) different than "me," "me," "me" (and so on).

13. *Destroys free will.* By declaring "the way," free will is abandoned in favor of frozen judgments that support your way, and only your way, of thinking. Lateral, permissive, freer-wheeling thinking is kept in the dugout while the game is being played by a narrow-minded set of rules that support the bigoted, confining thinking of the all-that-is-seen-is-red person.

Instead of going off half emotionally cocked, flipping your wig, or raising the roof with anger, it would be better to give peace a try by:

- Purposefully lowering your voice when addressing areas of concern.
- Considering the possibility that there might be some truth to what others are saying.
- Considering that you may be practically all wrong and others nearly all right.
- Soliciting rather than trying to squelch others' views.
- Accepting that others may not be nearly as interested as you in your way of thinking.
- Asking others what their opinion is rather than telling them what you think it "should" be.
- Actively summarizing your understanding of what the other is saying *and* the feeling you sense the other has about the content of their message before you exercise your jaws to even consider contrasting your views with theirs.

- Inquiring with "What do *you* think" messages. Asking people their opinion helps to neutralize possible anger about what the distinctions in beliefs are between the two of you.
- Minimizing rigid demands that block alternatives, that is, "should," "must," "have to," "got to," "supposed to," and "ought to."
- Sidestepping exaggerating speech, for example, "You never agree with me," "You always contradict me," and "Every time I try and tell you something you disagree."
- Expressing disappointment but not absolute horror about differences of opinion between you and others. Avoid statements such as "It's terrible that your thinking is so extreme," "It's awful you don't agree with me on this important matter," and "I can't stand it when you insinuate that I'm wrong."
- Accepting that although people are different, these differences need not angrily be made to clash and that individuals can unangrily agree to disagree.
- Admitting that when you state your position while angry, it would be advisable that you leave margin for the error that practically always accompanies an angry state of mind. Own the fact that what you think is gospel has by its very angry nature some thinking loopholes.
- Seeing that about the best anger can do and has repeatedly done throughout human history is to take a difficult, friction-dominated situation and make it worse by (a) fueling up the individuals' angry fires by practicing and building upon angry expressions, and (b) having the net effect of soliciting others to join in their anger attire.
- Emphasizing control and seeing that the negative effects of anger are overestimated, and that more harm has been done by anger expression than by anger restraint. If you read the front page of the newspaper, you can plainly

see that what the world can use more of is anger restraint, not anger expression.

Just as it's better to light one candle than to curse the darkness, so too in understanding and overcoming anger it is more fruitful to get past the fiery red of anger so as to see the light of the emotionally sane day. By getting more rational light on the subject in the form of logic, reason, and constructive rather than destructive action, you can begin to lighten up and to take more lightly various transgressions and inconveniences leveled against you. Such enlightenment can make the issue of dispute that much lighter and your higher tolerance for it more emotionally uplifting.

Note. From *You Can Control Your Anger! 21 Ways To Do It* by Bill Borcherdt. Copyright © 2000, Professional Resource Exchange, Inc., P.O. Box 15560, Sarasota, FL 34277-1560.

Chapter 4 Review Questions

1. Why is it nearly impossible to think reasonably and logically when angry?

2. What do you believe to be the main disadvantage of anger?

3. How is anger a self-righteous emotion?

4. Provide an example from this chapter that is especially becoming for overcoming anger.

5. How does anger destroy free-will?

CHAPTER 5

Without a Change of Thought, Anger Control Is for Naught: Anger Expressions as Child's Play

From age 2 to 102, by far the most common way of dealing with anger is to express it, express it, and express it some more until somehow magic occurs, and poof! it evaporates. As a consequence, a seeming Band-Aid is put on anger, but major surgery goes undone. This hydraulic theory of expression comes up short of permanent corrective action. Its child's-play suggestions include expression in the following ways:

- In no uncertain terms aggressively tell off the person you have made yourself angry at.
- Assertively disinhibit yourself without the aggressive antics above. Tell the other how you feel without telling him or her off.
- Vigorously and angrily hit a pillow.
- Yell and scream at the top of your lungs in an effort to reduce tension.
- Write out your angry feelings including what and/or whom they are directed toward.
- Envision yourself relaxing by the ocean and your angry feelings released out onto the tide.

- Express your anger toward those who, though not in your presence, you believe to be the source of your problems, for example, tell your parents off as if they were there.
- Exercise strenuously in hopes of lowering anger's temperature.
- Divert your anger with humor, that is, pretend that who you're angry at is Big Bird and rehearse in your fantasies expressing your anger toward that person as Big Bird.
- Imagine bad things happening to your adversary and escalate how angrily gleeful you feel about the other's misfortunes.
- Strenuously engage in other activities that may temporarily distract you from your bitterness, such as a hobby or special project.
- Throw darts at a picture of the person you're angry at.
- If you live with the person you are angry at, you can slush his or her toothbrush in the toilet bowl (when he or she is not looking, of course).
- Paint or draw pictures in a way that vents your anger.
- Perform target practice with a gun, imagining the target to be the person you despise.
- Harshly gossip, starting vicious rumors about the person at whom you are angry.
- Booby trap your opponent; for example, unplug one of the spark plugs in his or her car; pull his or her chair back as he or she is about to be seated; or eat the leftovers in the refrigerator that you know he or she was looking forward to eating.
- Publicly ridicule them by revealing unpleasant things about them when others are around.
- Be unkind toward them in other, more subtle ways, for example, make it a point not to greet them, say "no" to practically all their requests, talk gruffly to them, frown about opinions they have, act unreliably by not following through with prior mutual agreements, avoid eye con-

tact, glare at them in silent opposition, look out the window when they are talking to you, sigh when they voice their viewpoint, purposefully talk loudly so as to verbally drown them out, and mock or make fun of their shortcomings.

As you can see, anger expression comes in various sizes and shapes. Some tactics are relatively harmless, others not. However, all methods of anger expression, no matter how subtle and smooth an expression you opt for, have one common ingredient: they all qualify as child's play. This is because while they unreflectively express anger, the beliefs that caused the anger aren't changed. Like a child at play giving vent to his or her distaste for another's conduct, there is inevitably a backlash in word or deed for ungracious treatment; for example: "You called me a name so I will call you one too"; "You threw mud at me so I will sling some at you"; and "You tattled on me so I'll tattle on you" (all twice as bad, of course).

When adults mirror childish ("you did it first"), retaliatory, get even ("I'll show you") antics they focus more on getting their anger out so as to harm the other. Such 2-year-oldism, monkey-see-monkey do expressions fail to identify:

(a) the fact that their anger is caused by their demanding, intolerant, exaggerating beliefs;
(b) precisely what self-explanatory sentences are propelling anger. As a result, the child matinée continues. Mudslinging, name calling, hitting below the belt, getting a bead on and going for the jugular vein reach epidemic proportions - unless of course you learn that anger is not externally caused and that immature insistences that you be the one person on this green earth who gets what he or she wants each time he or she demands it can be uprooted.

Examples of childish, angry, out-of-control self-statements contrasted with mature anger-control coping ideas include:

CHILDISH OUT-OF-CONTROL SELF-STATEMENTS THAT WILL UNLEASH ANGER	MATURE ANGER-CONTROL COPING STATEMENTS
"It's mine because I wanted it first."	"True, I wanted it first, but it could just as well belong to the person who wanted it before me."
"Who does he think he is?"	"I know who he is and he is subject to the same rights and privileges that I am."
"She doesn't know what she is talking about from Adam."	"Maybe I don't know everything. I'm talking like I think I do."
"I have every right to throw mud in his eye or otherwise disrupt his foolish line of thinking."	"Maybe it would be better to listen more closely before I pass judgment on what I think I'm hearing - heaven forbid I might learn something!"
"I'll show her a thing or two."	"As I try to force-feed her with a thing or two, about the only thing I'll show and have to show for it is trouble."
"I'll fix his wagon."	"As I attempt to fix wagons, I break relationships."
"Take this!" (verbal and/or physical reprimand).	"Better that I keep my altercations to myself, because as I administer them there well may result a backlash or boomerang effect."
"I'll give her a dose of her own medicine."	"I may end up needing medicine with that kind of uncivilized attitude."
"He is always at fault (and is to be blamed because of it)."	"Better that I keep looking for my part in the plot if I want the situation rectified."
"She's a dummy."	"I think she is in error."

CHILDISH OUT-OF-CONTROL SELF-STATEMENTS THAT WILL UNLEASH ANGER *(Cont'd)*	MATURE ANGER-CONTROL COPING STATEMENTS *(Cont'd)*
"He's stupid."	"I think that he may be mistaken."
"She should know better."	"I would do well to realize that she likely isn't going to change - nor must she!"
"You started it."	"Regardless of who started it, how can I finish it in a manner that no one will get hurt?"
"You're getting under my skin."	"I'm letting myself overreact and then blaming it on someone else."
"I remember when he did very wrong by me and as far as I am concerned, he can rest in peace - real soon."	"I remember when he did very wrong by me - so?"
"Don't you dare look at me that way."	"So he gives me the evil eye, why is that so evil?"

Without a change of thought from childish, vindictive thinking to a more mature, tolerant perspective, anger will continue to poison personal and interpersonal objectives. Childlike objections block mature objectives. The paradox is that most of what is blown out of proportion and charges anger usually lacks cosmic significance. Many of the things that humans anger themselves about are not essential, necessary issues and items. They are common, everyday frustrations that are not too small to be blown out of proportion. Following are some examples of rational approaches to common frustrations using these symbols:

PM = Typical petty molehills (PM) that humans continue to insist that they mountain-climb over.

FT = The faulty thinking (FT) that produces the mountain-climbing anger overreaction.

CC = Countering cognitions (CC) that reduce anger.

BR = One behavioral recommendation (BR), because the best way to change an irrational cognition is to act against it.

RC = Rational commentary (RC).

PM 1:   *Being and admitting to being in the wrong.*

FT: "I absolutely must prove that I'm right and he or she is wrong. Being right is sacred; being in the wrong and admitting to it is to be avoided at costs."

CC: "Humans are sometimes right, sometimes wrong. I'm human, so why can't I too be sometimes right and sometimes wrong?"

BR: Purposefully admit to mistakes made 10 times in the next 24 hours.

RC: Angry-expressing people haven't learned that it is a sign of strength to admit your mistakes and that you can learn from them if you first acknowledge that you have committed them.

PM 2:   *Not being understood.*

FT: "I absolutely need to be understood by everyone in my social group and I cannot stand it when I'm not."

CC: "I've been misunderstood before and will likely be again. Each time I have been able to defend the onslaught of misunderstanding, and I think I can maintain my good track record."

BR: Going into the conversation, make a plan to dialogue with people who you realize are unlikely to understand why you view things as you do.

RC: To prevent anger build-up, realize and accept the fact that it is highly unlikely that anyone will ever understand you anywhere near as well as you do.

PM 3:   *Deficiencies in cooperation from associates.*

FT: "Others should cooperate with me, especially if I bend over backwards to do so with them."

CC: "Others decide whether they choose to cooperate with me; my choice is whether I will hassle them about their decision."

BR: Go out of your way to cooperate with others who you are fairly certain will not cooperate back with you; decide ahead of time that you will not anger yourself as they exercise their prerogative.

RC: Others are basically for their conveniences, not usually against yours, and will randomly sometimes cooperate with you and other times not. Understanding this can neutralize your anger.

PM 4:   *Others' disagreement.*

FT: "I explicitly need others to agree with me, and it is catastrophic when they don't."

CC: "Agreement from others, especially those who are close to me, is a great thing, but my life does not depend on such favoritism."

BR: Willfully disagree with someone when you know that such conflict will cost you a falling out from another's liking.

RC: In that you live with your decisions, see that the way you appraise matters is more important than how others do.

PM 5:   *Others' disapproval.*

FT: "I by necessity need others' approval, so they must give it to me. When they don't, they emotionally destroy me and are therefore responsible for my destruction. I despise them for what they have done to me."

CC: "Living in a social group makes others' approval desirable for reasons of social lubrication, but life does not come to a screeching halt without it."

BR: Purposefully act out of character in a way that will likely meet with the disapproval of some, and don't anger yourself when you receive a disapproving backlash. (But don't do something that will violate the law or cause you to lose your job, marriage, etc.)

RC: If you think you need and depend on others' approval, you are likely to make yourself angry at them and/or yourself when you are unable to gain it.

PM 6:   *Not being appreciated for your kind efforts.*

FT: "When I cater to others, they should cater back to me. Damn them when they don't complete the one-hand-washes-the-other equation."

BR: Do things for others that are kind and considerate, and that nobody will find out about.

RC: Make yourself less vulnerable to gaining others' acknowledgments by concentrating on the redeeming value of what kind acts you're doing rather than on whether others are recognizing your efforts.

PM 7:   *Achievement for achievement's sake.*

FT: "I must be fully accomplished and achieving in everything that I (attempt to) do - or else I'm no damned good."

CC: "Achievement is a great thing, especially when it is accompanied by advantages that enrich my life; such accomplishment is extra nice but not essential - especially to my being able to accept myself."

BR: Engage in fewer achieving, competitive acts and more informal, fun activities.

RC: Work to achieve, but make sure your accomplishments enable you to gain the resources to live a fuller, more satisfying, happier existence; otherwise, you may make yourself angry at yourself for working at goals that lack self-interest and have no end in sight.

PM 8:   *Communication deficiencies with significant others.*

FT: "I need important people in my life to communicate openly and frequently with me. If they really loved me they would; in the meantime, they make me angry when they don't."

CC: "Just because I love someone doesn't mean they are required to talk extensively to me nor does it necessarily mean they don't love me when they act in tight-lipped ways."

BR: Approach others in a nondesperate manner to explain that what is on their mind is important to you. See if you can't get them to commit to unbuttoning their thoughts and opinions to you more often.

RC: A dire need for communication from another results in loss of bargaining power in the relationship and puts your happiness at the mercy of whether others decide to converse with you or not.

PM 9:   *Lack of acceptance, a surplus of rejection from others.*

FT: "I'm nobody until somebody accepts me, so when others reject me they belittle me and cause me much hurt."

CC: "My emotional life does not rely on whether others like and accept me, though I consider their acceptance to be an emotional advantage."

BR: Repeatedly approach those who may not accept you and see whether your disapproval anxiety diminishes as you extend yourself into disapproving social territory more frequently.

RC: Understand that some people will not accept you for the same reasons that others will and that others' dislikes for you are representative of their tastes rather than of you.

PM 10:   *Losing out in love.*

FT: "I must get the love that I need from the same people who I need it from."

CC: "Others will decide whether they love me. Just as I don't need their love, I need not anger myself at them or me when they don't deliver."

BR: Audition many potential love partners and see that sometimes you will be successful and sometimes you won't in garnering love. See that if you don't experiment, you will likely never succeed.

RC: In and out of love, those who succeed fail the most but persist more - even when it seems against odds to do so.

PM 11:   *Lack of recognition for your efforts, credentials, and accomplishments.*

FT: "Others should recognize me as the credentialized, high-achieving person that I am, and it does more than perturb me when they don't."

CC: "I need not make myself out to be an achievement junkie and desperately depend on others to provide me with heavy doses of notoriety."

BR: Continue to perform well but make it a point to hide your abilities under a bushel rather than expose them, hoping that others will take notice. Do this until you can take or leave the recognition factor.

RC: Accomplishing to gain attention can lead to emotionally shallow successes generating a bottomless pit syndrome, that is, how much attention from your social group is enough?

PM 12:   *Lacking immediate comfort.*

FT: "I'm in this world to feel comfortable and at all times I must; damn the world when it does not make these provisions of ease with ease."

CC: "I'm in the world to experience the world, and that will likely include a fair amount of discomfort."

BR: Place yourself in situations where you typically make yourself feel uncomfortable and keep doing so until familiarity blunts its terrors; for example, public speaking, asking for a date, or voicing your opinion at a staff meeting.

RC: Many of the things that are to our advantage to do are not comfortable to do in the short run but can be in the long run. Present pain for future gain allows for a longer range, more rational perspective than the reality that the pleasure of the moment often leads to pain later on.

PM 13: *Others overlooking apologizing for their wrongdoing.*

FT: "Others should know enough to apologize for their mistakes, and I have a right to resent them until they do."

CC: "It is not for me to determine another's apology; it is my decision to anger myself when they don't express regret for their errors."

BR: Seek out the wrongdoer's thoughts about his or her mistake. If you choose to, nondemandingly express your interest in being apologized to.

RC: Others' apologies may or may not include an indication of a plan to correct their insensitivities in the future. You need not depend on an apology to cushion your displeasure.

PM 14: *Incidents of unfairness and deficiencies of deservingness by life and/or others in it.*

FT: "I must get what I deserve, and life and others in it must provide same. When they don't I'll get even, even if it means undercutting my own long-range best interests."

CC: "I generally get what I get, often not what I think that I deserve."

BR: Talk to others about your perceived shortcomings in life and/or in others' provisions and explain how you plan on constructively dealing with such negligence.

RC: Be glad you don't always get what you deserve in life, because if you did, you may suffer from more disadvantages than you already do!

PM 15: *Minimal encouragement/emotional support from those who you deem to influence you.*

FT: "Others know full well that I depend on them for support. Therefore, it is their duty to provide me with reassurance - and heaven forbid my anger if and when they don't."

CC: "The best kind of reliance is self-reliance - something I can almost always inject into myself."

BR: Independently choose a project to embrace yourself in, determining prior to it that you are not, even in the least little bit, going to hint around for encouraging feedback.

RC: Self-encouragement is comforting when you take the time to understand that this is one of the things you can always do on your own behalf.

PM 16: *Being excluded; not being invited to attend with the group; or finding that your opinion related to group consensus is not being solicited.*

FT: "Others should always include me in their plans and consistently seek out my views on matters of group concern. I find it and them distasteful when they don't."

CC: "I am capable of standing on my own two emotional feet and do not require inclusion to do so."

BR: Do a trial run of intentionally excluding yourself from group plans and opinions, doing so in a non-resentful, unangry fashion.

RC: Exclusion from group activities can have the advantages of establishing yourself as chairman of the board with your own agenda.

PM 17: *Not knowing tomorrow's answers today.*

FT: "I need to know which of my choices is most accurate before deciding on path A or B."

CC: "I don't have to be the one person in the universe who has assured certainty and orderliness as part of his or her choices, nor do I have to anger myself when I'm inevitably not."

BR: When faced with a decision, give yourself 15 seconds to make it - and then develop a plan to live with it.

RC: Watch out for what you wish for, because you might get it. If you knew tomorrow's answers today, you would likely feel bored, lacking a vital sense of anticipation.

PM 18: *Near absence of praise, strokes, or compliments.*

FT: "I find praise from others to be mandatory for my work style, so others should praise me just as I stroke and compliment them."

CC: "I don't have to baby myself with requirements that others praise me for all or any of my efforts and successes, nor anger myself when I discover them to not be especially praiseful."

BR: Make it a point to find value in your own perfecting of your projects and the feelings of accomplishment that follow without seeking praise from your associates in terms such as, "What do you think of my masterpiece of all masterpieces?"

RC: The more you make yourself dependent on praise for your efforts, the more hurt and anger you are likely to give yourself when others come up short in this category.

PM 19:   *Parental faults that you have.*

FT: "Because I am the centerpiece of my child's life, I must do all of the right things in his or her rearing and get angrily down on myself when I don't."

CC: "I help to raise my child, but there are many other influences, most of which are beyond my control, including his or her genetic makeup."

BR: Share your parental insecurities with other parents while moving ahead with your own goals and ambitions.

RC: Understand the value of not defining yourself by your parenting. Use your parenting to work on your own mental health, largely by accepting yourself regardless of your parenting outcomes.

PM 20:   *Sexual flaws and inadequacies.*

FT: "I must be among the sexually perfect or else I'm perfectly sexless and worthless."

CC: "True, I can't do acrobats sexually or nonsexually, but all that means is that I'm a card-carrying member of the (im)perfect human race."

BR: Talk openly with your sexual partner about your shortcomings.

RC: Humans are imperfect in and out of sex, and it is unlikely that they will succeed at never failing in either case.

PM 21: *Others' harsh, unfair, crusty, or negative criticisms.*

FT: "Others must not unjustly criticize me, and I must fight angry fire with angry fire when they do."

CC: "Others have a right to be wrong, including to wrongfully criticize me."

BR: Go out of your way to be pleasant to critical-acting people in your life. This will likely neutralize some of your own animosity while making it difficult for your opposition to sustain anger.

RC: If you don't define or rate yourself or the other by their criticism of you, it is unlikely you will create anger toward yourself or the other party.

PM 22: *Gaps in general patronizing behaviors that otherwise help shape pleasant human interactions.*

FT: "I don't ask for much in terms of pleasant social discourse from others. Because I ask for so little - that is, pleasant greetings, others saying please and thank you, a smile now and then, a kinder and gentler tone of voice, asking if I can use some assistance with matters of importance to me, seeking out my opinion, defending me in conversation, finding some truth to my views about life - I should be granted what I so little ask for and expect."

CC: "Regardless of the amount of common courtesy I would appreciate, my associate is not required to provide such patronization. How much such patronization would warm the cockles of my heart is irrelevant."

BR: Patronize others a bit less yourself. To those that might overdo such daily accommodation, simply explain that going so far out of the way is not necessary.

RC: Patronize your social group enough so that they can easily recognize that you are with them rather than against them. Anything beyond that is not necessary.

Most of the happenings that humans make themselves antagonistic about don't have long-lasting significance. Like children who bicker about petty things, for example, "I'll bet that my Dad can beat up your Dad," individuals will more likely than not exaggerate the significance of what is considered to be a frustrating occurrence. Anger as child's play is like playing with fire, and in the end one is at high risk for being burned. Prevention of anger build-up means staying away from the emotional fire that is made to happen from feuds, conflicts, criticisms, and other unpleasantries. A change to rational thought will not go for naught when emotionally responding to life's sometimes nasty experiences. Anger-control efforts without a change to rational thought is like a cart without springs - jolted by every pebble in the road. Clearer thinking makes for a smoother ride - and I don't mean like one in your childhood little red wagon!

Chapter 5 Review Questions

1. What is meant by anger expression as being a Band-Aid solution?

2. What does "2-year-oldism" refer to in terms of anger control?

3. Do you agree that the best way to change an irrational idea is to act against it?

4. Why is it that anger can be considered "child's play?"

5. How is it that the hydraulic theory of anger expression comes up short in correcting the problem?

CHAPTER 6

Asking Yourself 50 Therapeutic Questions And Giving Yourself 50 Therapeutic Answers: Becoming Your Own Best Anger-Control Therapist

Alfred Adler said, "It's easier to fight for your ideals than it is to live up to them." How true. Good advice is certainly easier to give than it is to follow, but unless you start with sound, scientific self-advice, the self-help project is unlikely to get off the ground. Also, good advice is good advice and has potential value if put to use, no matter how difficult it might be to do so. This chapter is designed to invite and encourage you to maneuver yourself into asking, answering, and giving follow-up attention to questions that will represent you not only fighting for your anger-control ideas but also living up to them so as to teach yourself to become your own best advisor.

Humans are responsible for their own emotions. You can exercise that responsibility by asking yourself the right questions and giving yourself the correct answers that will be of major assistance in disintegrating angry tendencies. The benefits of the 50-part anti-anger questionnaire to follow can best be achieved by first ruling out cop-out philosophies that detract from self-responsibility. Each of the following conclusions reflect "other blame," meaning that someone or something else allegedly causes anger or gives it to another. These irresponsible self-statements can be challenged by more responsible assertions as in the following illustrations.

IRRESPONSIBLE, OTHER-BLAMING IDEAS	COUNTERING, RESPONSIBILITY-FOR-SELF, NO-BLAME POSITIONS
"He made me angry."	"I made myself angry."
"It got me upset."	"I upset myself."
"My family disturbed me."	"I disturbed myself about my family."
"She shouldn't upset me like that."	"Better that I not upset myself."
"That bummed me out."	"I bummed myself out."
"What a bummer."	"What a bummer I make it out to be."
"Now that's something that gets me mad."	"Now that is something that I get myself mad about."
"They get under my skin."	"I let them get under my skin."
"Sticks, stones, and words harm me."	"I sharpen sticks, stones, and words up and hurt myself in the process (as I stick them in myself.)"
"That's the way it goes."	"That's the way I make it go."
"I fell off the wagon."	"I pushed myself of the wagon."
"That really gets my cork."	"I really allow my cork to go off."
"That gets my goat."	"I get my own goat."
"He made me pop a cork."	"I popped my own cork."
"He really lathered me up this time."	"I lather myself up every time (I overreact)."
"Alcohol and other drugs did me in."	"I did myself in with alcohol and other drugs."

Unless irrational-irresponsible ideas are uprooted, anger-control methods will be difficult to plant. Alternative beliefs that prevent the overreactions and personalizations that are at the core of anger had best be identified. Getting at the jugular vein of your anger and doing major surgery on your angry inclinations can be accomplished by using the following three-part self-analysis that is comprised of a list of therapeutic questions (TQ) to ask yourself; examples of therapeutic answers (TA) designed to lighten the angry load; and rational comments (RC) that reflect further on the question under consideration.

TQ 1:   *"What does 'compassion begins at home' mean for me?"*

TA: "It means it is to my advantage to get after my anger, to reprimand it but to not get after or condemn myself for having it - in short, to condemn the sin but not the sinner."

RC: A huge mistaken assumption is that prior to correcting a mistake you must blame someone for making it. On the contrary, if you rate yourself as a bad person because of your errors, you will likely commit more of them.

TQ 2:   *"What does 2-year-oldism mean for me?"*

TA: "It refers to my acting like a child when I don't get my own way, resulting in my making myself into a well-practiced baby."

RC: Taffy is nice but not necessary. There are better ways to express disappointment about not getting it than to whine and scream when baby doesn't get his or her milk. Such childlike activity demonstrates an immature protest against reality; a refusal to accept what exists. Self-stating "tough beans!" in times of deprivation will break this childish inclination to contest being dealt a bad hand, opening up the option of playing a bad hand good.

TQ 3:   *"Do I think that others have the right to intention-*
           ally act badly toward me?"
TA: "Due to free will and human limitations, others can
           choose to purposefully send barbs in my direction;
           they do not require permission to do so."
RC: Others have free choice, which often may not be our
           choice. However, as they have a right to try to dis-
           advantage us, we have a right (preferably exercising
           it in an unangry fashion) to protect ourselves by cre-
           ating a temporary distance between them and us.

TQ 4:   *"What does dousing rather than fanning the flames*
           of anger mean for me?"
TA: "It means acting on my own behalf to better regu-
           late, curtail, and put boundaries on my creating my
           own anger."
RC: Nip anger in the bud by having more tolerant, ac-
           cepting forgiving philosophies on the tip of your
           tongue. They can be pressed into action when tempted
           to throw gasoline on disappointing events or others'
           annoying antics.

TQ 5:   *"What does dissolving rather than expressing or re-*
           pressing anger mean for me?"
TA: "It refers to the idea of chasing down the thinking
           that produced the anger, abolishing that thinking
           pattern, and substituting methods of thought that
           will abolish/evaporate anger rather than dramati-
           cally expressing it or not acknowledging it in a make-
           believe fashion."
RC: A majority of anger-control consumers are instructed
           toward extremism: Either let anger all hang out by
           expressing it or suffocate yourself by stuffing anger
           so as not to rock the boat. Unless one studies REBT,
           the third option of identifying and ripping apart the

philosophical roots of anger is not offered. I have helped hundreds of clients to extinguish anger more permanently by teaching them to think differently and more tolerantly about this old, intolerant problem. Many clients are pleasantly surprised that they can (often) quickly learn to unshackle anger by addressing their anger-producing thinking.

_TQ 6:_   *"What does it mean for me that anger expression produces rather than reduces anger?"*

TA: "When you practice a bad habit such as anger expression, you make yourself more angry. As I rehearse my angry exhibitions, I strengthen anger as the sideshow that it is. I make myself more angry because with practice I strengthen my condemning, demanding, punitive views that insist that others be just like me and that the world cater to me, me, me, and me only. Far better that I lay off such self-centeredness so as to expand my tolerance level."

RC: Expressing anger indiscriminately, without spot checking and changing the irrational ideas that caused your upset to begin with, will sharpen your anger-expression skills and dull your relationships with others. Such free expression will likely result in your feelings of anger going out the back door and coming in the front with an added boomerang effect produced from the momentum that has built up from your practicing a bad habit made worse by repetition.

_TQ 7:_   *"What does undamning acceptance mean for me, and how can its philosophy assist me in destroying my anger before it destroys me?"*

TA: "This concept allows me to more fully accept myself, others, and life rather than to condemn each for their shortcomings. Consequently, my relationships with all three will likely be made to be more pleasantly lubricated."

RC: The word that highlights mental health and emotional well-being more than any other is acceptance. Accepting people and circumstances as they exist, rather than protesting against their being the way they are, resolves conflict and dissolves the interfering angry emotions that are so often made to occur.

TQ 8:   *"Define for yourself the difference between angry and unangry restraint."*

TA: "Angry restraint refers to rightly restraining yourself on the outside but wrongly angering yourself on the inside. Unangry restraint is a more preferable solution to emotional self-control in that I not only restrain myself on the outside but also increase my tolerance level on the inside by not secretly condemning who or what I am restraining my anger from. Instead, I not so secretly build a case for acceptance and forgiveness."

RC: Anger-control artists can sometimes make themselves into con artists by fooling themselves into believing that because they have restrained expression of anger, they have gotten rid of this hardened emotion. Restraint plus damning and condemning another under your breath does not constitute a very high-level solution to anger control. You may eliminate the expression of anger, but that doesn't do away with anger's existence. You may see restraint, but what you may still get is anger.

TQ 9:   *"What does 'Nobody in human history has ever pissed another off' mean for me?"*

TA: "It means that there is no magic in life; that no one can access my gut and give me anger. Others can

RC: displease me to seeming no end, but only I can go for the displeasing bait and piss myself off!"

Neither happiness nor unhappiness is externally caused. Admitting that you trip your own trigger with your own impatient low frustration tolerance and/or self- or other-blame is a significant factor. Without a philosophy of admittance as to your accountability for your own anger, the overactive problem will go untouched. This question is a constant bone of contention by many people who often go to their graves kicking, screaming, and insisting that (a) others do so get them angry, (b) others must change their annoying ways, and (c) until those others change they will remain eternally angry (due to the faults of others).

TQ 10: *"What does 'Anger as an overreaction will boomerang on me' mean for me?"*

TA: "It refers to the idea that anger is philosophically based. Unless the thinking that originated the angry feelings is done away with, my overreactions will come back to haunt me because I still won't have come to terms with my original infantile beliefs from which anger erupts."

RC: Unless you learn the trigger point of anger - demandingness - and how to dismantle it, anger will linger, eventually coming back at you with an even fuller force. A philosophy of challenging yourself to prevent the first-level overreaction of anger by dissipating the insistences that set it off is a more comprehensive method for anger resolution. Getting at anger before it gets out of the starting block stops anger before it has an opportunity to begin.

TQ 11: *"What does 'Anger is a damnation of others' mean for me?"*

TA: "A prerequisite for feeling anger toward another is that you think less of that person prior to expressing your fury. If I tried to feel angry toward another without exposing damnation I would be hard put to do so."

RC: To damn another human being is essential if your goal is to create anger on the inside about something you are annoyed with on the outside. Without this central ingredient of damnation of others, you have anger licked - before it licks you.

TQ 12: *"Why do I sometimes think it's easier to believe that others have a right to be wrong than that this person (with whom I associate on a regular basis) has a right to be wrong?"*

TA: "Talk is cheap, even at the suggested retail price. It seems easier to forgive others for their trespasses when I am not routinely exposed to their faults. Also, it is likely that out of my own grandiosity I sometimes believe that I should be the one person in the universe who is continually surrounded by others who have nothing better to do than to please me. Last, 'others' has a distant ring to it, while 'this person' has a more immediate implication, implying that when speaking about the latter I will be expected to roll up my sleeves and go to work to accept the reality of others' right to be wrong - a reality that requires much work of the kind that I make myself allergic to."

RC: Realities that hit closer to home are often more difficult to deal with. Good advice is easier to give than to follow. It is easier to advise oneself on the fact that people whom you don't know - but not *this* person, whom you do know - have a right to be wrong. Humans frequently convince themselves that they are special (rather than unique) and due to such a self-proclaimed form of anointment conclude that those with whom they associate on a steady basis have no right to violate the terms of such a crowning - though those abstractly from afar do have a right to err.

TQ 13: *"Do I/must I learn from my mistakes?"*

TA: "Although there is no universal law that I have to learn from my mistakes, it would be to my advantage to try like hell to do so."

RC: A client once said to me, "Bill, when I come back to see you next time, promise that I won't have made the same mistake again - I'll make a new one." What a roundabout way of learning from one's mistakes! If you believe it is a necessity to not make the same mistake more than once, you will likely put yourself down when you do. If you think it makes little difference whether or not you opt for correction, you will continue to goof and further disadvantage yourself. It is better to learn from mistakes, because you will likely be better off; but because of humans free-will, they do not have to do what is preferable, desirable, or better.

TQ 14: *"What does 'Most people are for themselves rather than against me' illustrate for me?"*

TA: "It points to the idea that practically all those whom I will meet in my lifetime have better things to do than to purposefully try to do me in."

RC: Understanding this interpersonal equation can neutralize hostility otherwise encouraged by this often faulty inference. A nondefensive approach to others underlies the therapeutic answer to this balanced question.

TQ 15:   *"What do I think is meant by 'Anger expression usually increases frustration'?"*

TA: "Many of my frustrating experiences, especially with others, don't change that much, so the more I express anger about these matters that don't change, the more frustration mounts."

RC: Few people find self-change to be a project they find interesting, exciting, or challenging. A quick review of your friends, family, and work and other associates will likely document this somewhat pessimistic reality. To command change when little to none is forthcoming is to breed hopelessness and increase frustration.

TQ 16:   *"What is my view of 'Acting out of control as a means of gaining control is contradictory'?"*

TA: "Just as I wouldn't throw gasoline instead of water on a fire to put it out, neither would I want to act like a 2-year-old to achieve emotional maturity."

RC: Acting out of control breeds additional infantilism, not adulthood. It is a contradiction in terms and behavior to decrease anger by increasing its out-of-control drama.

TQ 17:   *"How can I interpret for myself the notion that 'Anger stems from my philosophy of life.'"*

TA: "This means that *I* am responsible for my angry feelings due to my flawed philosophies/beliefs about what life's disappointments mean for me."

RC: Humans largely or mainly feel the way they think. Change your thinking in a more rational direction and you will likely feel better. Identify thoughts that prevent anger, and this will allow you the freedom to choose other, healthier feelings.

TQ 18: "*What are my thoughts about anger being more a sign of strength or a sign of weakness?*"

TA: "I think anger represents weakness, insecurity, fear, and personal unsurety."

RC: Angry-acting people are really fearful people because they are afraid that others can demean or put them down. They use anger as a mechanism of control in a feeble effort to gain the likings of others, which they believe they require. Once they realize that these arbitrary requirements - approval, understanding, and love acceptance - are nonessential, they are better able to back away from anger as reflected in their own fears and insecurities.

TQ 19: "*What is my opinion of the idea that 'What you see is anger, but what you get is hurt'?*"

TA: "Anger disguises hurt because, as a seemingly more powerful emotion, it is latched on to as an alternative to the more feeble feeling states of self-blame, self-pity, and self-depreciation that are incorporated into the anatomy of hurt."

RC: Anger invigorates, but hurt deflates emotions, taking the wind out of your emotional sails. The hurtful disguise behind anger's smokescreen may never be dealt with due to its being overshadowed by anger's high wind.

TQ 20: "*What do I think is meant by 'If you don't get yourself angry you will become someone else's doormat' - and do I agree?*"

TA: "I strongly disagree, because there are many more civilized ways to prevent others from figuratively walking all over me. Using the bullyish, angry tactics of those who try to take advantage of me only manufactures added hostility and bitterness which will likely result in me conducting myself in the same childish ways of my adversaries."

RC: Protecting yourself with philosophies and tactics that reflect logic and reason in the service of your emotions and behavior is a less strenuous and more healthy and helpful approach to protecting yourself from others' wrath. Clearheadedness ordinarily precedes creativity in protection-of-self methods.

TQ 21:   *"Do I agree with the notion 'If I get rid of the need, I get rid of my anger'?"*

TA: "I believe that angry people are really fearful in that they believe they need certain advantages from others, such as acceptance, approval, agreement, understanding, and so on, and so they kick anger into gear to control for what they wrongly think they need. Evaporate the need and you rid three disturbances at the same time: emotional dependency (neediness), fear, and anger."

RC: Being at least relatively emotionally sound requires that you not stretch your rational desires, wants, wishes, and preferences into irrational "NEEDS." The less you view others' favoritism toward you as bigger than life, the higher level emotional life you will create. Something may be good and you may want it, but that is a far cry from needing it.

TQ 22:   *"What do I make out of the idea 'Reprimand your wrongful behavior, but don't reprimand yourself'?"*

TA: "I deem it to mean there is value to judging my behavior but it is self-defeating to judge myself by my behavior."

RC: If you don't admit to and evaluate your wrongdoing, you will likely continue to make the same mistake over and over again. If you acknowledge your error and condemn yourself for it, you will also be more likely to goof repeatedly. As this principle pertains to saying good riddance to anger, the less angry you make yourself for overreacting, the less likely you will be to overreact in the future. Also, when you don't judge yourself, the better able you will be to not judge others for their misbehavior, which will help to dissolve the damnation component of anger.

TQ 23:   *"Do I believe that its easy or difficult to get myself angry?"*

TA: "In the short run it seems easier to get myself angry because of the often suddenness of the feeling, but picking up the often leftover emotional debris - such as broken relationships, lost jobs, physical complications, or legal problems - tells me that anger expression is the hard part and restraint is the easy part - over the course of a lifetime, that is."

RC: Looking beyond your nose, beyond the immediacy of anger, safely reveals that anger expression is the difficult and dangerous route to take. Human history with its wars and rumors of wars, as well as the front page of the newspaper as it reflects man's inhumanity to man, unfortunately illustrates the hypothesis that anger is difficult, *not* easy.

TQ 24:   *"Is anger a good way for me to express a message?"*

TA: "Anger is an exceptionally poor way for me to express what I have to say because (a) others will hear my fervor but not my facts, and (b) I strengthen my angry thunder and lightening approach to interpersonal (in)effectiveness."

RC: Booming out your words will "freeze" others' receptive ears, resulting in a cold chill response to your message. A thunder-and-lightning approach to communication may well knock out the wires that carry your point of view. The noise box increases, destroying the fuse box from which conversation originates.

TQ 25: *"Do I believe that anger is a form of 'navel staring'?"*

TA: "When I make myself angry I am accelerating my view and my view only; consequently I get myself hung up on one way: my way. The phrase 'navel staring' is a good metaphor for such self-centered antics."

RC: Angry-acting people display their self-righteousness by how they insist on how right they are and how ungodly wrong you are. They stare at their own opinions, pigheadedly refusing to consider others.

TQ 26: *"Do I agree that if I don't express my anger, it will backfire on me?"*

TA: "On the contrary! I believe that if I *do* express my anger it will backfire on me."

RC: Until you discard the faulty thinking that causes anger, you will strengthen and multiply the anger habit via expression. Emotional corruption will increase as you practice expressing anger; the more you express, the more an overexpressor you cause yourself to be.

TQ 27: *"Do I agree that I have basically two choices about what to do with anger: either express it or stockpile it - sweep it under the rug, so to speak?"*

TA: "Better that I consider a third alternative seldom recognized by others, unless they have privy to Rational Emotive Behavior Therapy (REBT): dissolving this evil emotion. I can accomplish this by modifying my philosophy of life in a way that better accommodates a more accepting, tolerant view of unfairness and injustice."

RC: Anger-expression (usually unreflectively) advocates have had the market on what to do with anger, with a "let it all hang out" mentality sitting in the front row as the solution to controlling it. Consequently, the jugular vein of anger's origin - the individual's personal belief system about what it means to be inconvenienced or selected against - continues to be rehearsed. These beliefs reflect demands, exaggerations, and self- or other-judgments. Only with the onset of cognitive-behavior therapy, with Dr. Albert Ellis, originator of REBT and "grandfather of cognitive-behavior therapy" taking the lead in instructing a more philosophical alternative, that this third option has been exposed. Still, it sometimes seems like an uphill battle to educate therapists and the general public alike that this third alternative can serve as an enduring means of killing anger before it stiffens you.

TQ 28: *"Am I compatible with the notion that because anger feels good for a period of time, it is therefore good for me?"*

TA: "It is true that anger has its feel-good, addictive enticements and that when something feels good there is usually a longing to go back to it. But if anger is such a good thing, why, I'd best ask myself, does it hurt so bad?"

RC: Many things and events feel good but in the end are detrimental to your best interests. Smoking cigarettes, excessive use of alcohol, overeating, and accelerating your car beyond a safe speed all feel good but do not qualify as experiences that contribute to your long-range best interests.

TQ 29: *"Do I believe that, given continued highly frustrating circumstances, feeling anger is inevitable?"*

TA: "I believe that difficult circumstances, with their mounds of frustration, convenience anger but that I have free-will and can determine for myself if I wish to act on this convenience item and produce anger."

RC: Humans have the capacity to tolerate anything as long as they are alive - including seeming never-ending frustration. When they convince themselves of that fact they put themselves in a more strategic position to "put up their dukes" against anger.

TQ 30:   *"What in my own mind is the difference between annoyance, irritation, displeasure, and anger?"*

TA: "Simply put, there are differences; the biggest relates to the invaluable distinction between preference and demand."

RC: To preferentially want others to treat us fair and square will produce annoyance, irritation, and displeasure when others trespass on such interpersonal desires; to be demandingly insistent, that is, "Others *must* do well by me," leap-frogs into anger. Anger does not blend in with these other three emotions; it is distinctive and autonomous. Whether you produce anger or these other three is determined by whether you are thinking in the role of the preferrer or the demander.

TQ 31:   *"Do I believe that anger is a good method of persuasion?"*

TA: "With anger what you mainly see is red and what you primarily feel is despisement. What others feel is your anger begetting their anger or possibly fear of you. It's difficult to persuade someone who feels anger and/or fear toward you."

RC: Let's pretend that, as a result of your anger and others' intimidation by it, you are able to induce others to at least temporarily act according to your persuasion. Still, after they have left your presence they are likely to not only disclaim your point of view all over again but to unload on you in varying passive-aggressive ways. In the short run, anger can gain acclaim by fear and intimidation, but in the long run, disdain is likely to dominate. If you persuade as a porcupine, those to whom you administer angry persuasion are likely to sharply turn against you at their first opportunity.

TQ 32:   *"What are my thoughts regarding 'I have a right to feel anger, so I will exercise that right regardless of person, place, or thing'?"*

TA: "I think this presumption is quite accurate, but - do I really want to die with my rights on?"

RC: Only exercise your rights as they contribute to your long-range happiness and survival. Silence can be golden. Sometimes the best way to stand up for yourself is to take a conflictual matter sitting down. To be rational is to do what is in your best interests, and by angrily conducting yourself in a way that leads to you being on the outside of a job, friendship, or love relationship looking in, you are exercising your rights, but in an irrational, self-defeating way.

TQ 33:   *"Do I believe it true that when I work on my anger others should go out of their way to help me to do so by patronizing me more?"*

TA: "There is no evidence that others are required to do my work for me by making it easier for me to control my anger via finding the right ridge on my feet and licking it."

RC: Others are not duty bound to assist you or baby you at anger control. There are certain things that others can't do for us and that we can only do for ourselves, including controlling our emotions.

TQ 34:   *"Do I agree that anger is a good way to disinhibit and motivate myself?"*

TA: "I think anger is one way to motivate and disinhibit myself, but it is far from the only way and perhaps farther yet from the best way to do so."

RC: Motivation by anger often brings on destructive, aggressive expressions. Anger will get you out of the starting block, but it will often try to destroy others who are running toward the same finish line. There are more civilized, self-interested means of igniting incentive such as more fully appreciating long-range feelings of accomplishment of a job well done. Disinhibiting yourself minus the fury to match the effort is a more sane, sensible way of tasting different slices of life while generating energy to strive for your goals. About the only things that can be done with anger that can't be done without it are to harm or kill someone.

TQ 35:   *"Overall, would I say that anger has more advantages or more disadvantages?"*

TA: "It is quite obvious to me that whether it be between individuals, communities, or nations, anger may be fashionable but it is also foolhardy."

RC: Humans seem intent on harming if not killing each other off. It may well be curtains for the species unless rational ideas are applied, ideas that harness if not dissolve angry tendencies. To take the time to more fully appreciate the detrimental effects of anger and the advantages of keeping your cool is to provide a deterrent to giving vent to this explosive emotion.

TQ 36:   *"What does 'Anger is normal but not healthy' mean for me?"*

TA: "I interpret this to mean that most people, given the same unjust treatment, would make themselves angry; but what most people do is nothing to brag about."

RC: There is a major difference between "normal" and "healthy." To act as a rational nonconformist while realizing that you know better than anyone whether it is to your advantage to make yourself angry is to control anger rather than allow it to control you. Just because it is normal for "the tail to wag the dog," does not mean that if you work your tail off you can't constitute a majority of one in your social group and decide to do the redeeming healthy thing (not overreact to injustice) rather than the unredeeming unhealthy action (overreact to unfairness and undeservingness).

TQ 37:   *"What do I believe to be the meaning behind the phrase 'Anger is a human yet an inhumane thing to do'?"*

TA: "I believe it means that humans have powerful tendencies to come on angrily strong (weak) when frustrated, deprived, or inconvenienced - but the harm such "gangway" mentality provides also makes angry rituals inhumane."

RC: Anger is both for (in that it gives expression to a natural human tendency) and against humans (in that it can destroy them). This for-and-against notion can be resolved by angry-acting people getting off their high horse while unshackling themselves from the insistence that they, others, and life be different than they are in reality. To accept human life as it is lets loose of the inhumane while furthering the humane part of our existence.

TQ 38:   *"How can I examine and explain to myself what I believe is meant by 'playing God and fighting like the devil'?"*

TA: "I believe it to refer to two or more people who haven't yet learned to disagree and are each in turn behaving as holier-than-thou while believing the other is unworthier-than-all. I also believe that this phrase explains the majority of feuds and infantile ramblings that humans often take on."

RC: Self-righteous is a potential spark for anger. Godlike perspectives may allow one to feel all-powerful, but the fighting-like-hell aspect of the disagreement creates a hell-on-earth atmosphere, fit for the devil but not for civilized earthlings.

TQ 39:   *"How would I explain to myself the notion that anger isn't manufactured simply from observations of flawed conduct nor from the inferences that are made following such devilish activity?"*

TA: "It means that emotional disturbances such as anger aren't created by the adversity that occurred, nor by the inferred reasons or perceptions of why it occurred but rather by the irrational beliefs about the inferences."

RC: Humans observe injustices and experience mistreatment and then make inferences and form perceptions of what they observe, for example, that others are purposefully disadvantaging them, that someone's lack of follow through was intentional, or that a display of unkindness was the result of a willful act. These inferences, as disjointed and personalized as they might be, will not create anger. What will produce anger is the demand that others' blockages, whether purposeful or not, are beside the point and should, must, or ought not occur. There might be many reasons why someone acted neglectfully or badly other than intentionally doing so. To acknowledge such possibilities changes the inferences but will not uproot the cause of the anger disturbance; only uprooting the commanding irrational ideas will do that, that is, by accepting that others have a right to purposefully act badly, and furthermore, to not learn from their mistakes!

TQ 40:   *"What do I think is meant by the interesting statement that anger is a way of punishing yourself for the actions of others?"*

TA: "I think this statement refers to the idea that it is difficult to cling to anger toward another without harming yourself."

RC: By stewing, whining, self-pitying, engaging in excessive demandingness and controllingness, and other acting-out distasteful ingredients of anger, you are putting a lot of pressure on yourself. Such whimsical conduct will come back to haunt you with heightened tension and ongoing frustration when you discover that you are not the general manager of the universe after all.

TQ 41:   *"Do I believe anger to be a good or poor problem-solving method, and in either case, why?"*

TA: "Anger is a poor problem-solving method because, when in the throes of anger, your goal is likely to be to do the other person in rather than to solve the problem."

RC: Anger is anticollaborative, anticooperative, and anticompromise. These deficiencies as created by anger rob you of problem-solving capacities. Anger also causes tunnel vision and makes you unable to consider other alternatives that run counter to your way of thinking.

_TQ 42:_   *"What do I think the question 'How can fools learn from their mistakes?' means in reference to anger control?"*

TA: "I think it means that if you put yourself down (label yourself as a fool) for blowing off steam you will see yourself as a fool through and through and as a result will continue to act foolish in an angry fashion."

RC: The self-fulfilling promise is pressed into action when you judge yourself as a fool in that you basically tell and convince yourself that because you are such a fool you are only capable of continuing rather than learning from and eventually correcting your angry-acting mistakes.

_TQ 43:_   *"What do I believe is meant by the statement 'Some people will like you for the same reasons others will hate you' - and what are its implications for anger control?"*

TA: "To me it means that what others think and say about me illustrates their tastes and preferences, not me as a human being."

RC: Understanding that your way of being in this world is unique and that some will appreciate it and some won't can melt the angry defensiveness that often is made to accompany others' disfavored appraisals. Beauty, obscenities, humor, and what others think about us are all in the eyes of the beholder.

_TQ 44:_   *"How do I interpret the idea of 'bittersweet revenge,' and what is its place in anger extinction?"*

TA: "I believe it to mean the idea that revenge is sour rather than sweet. This is due to the complicating factors that set in when angry feelings are strengthened by revenge activity."

RC: If angry revenge is so sweet, why is the world in the 'from border to border' hostile shape that it is in? By more fully appreciating the fallout debris from resentment, you are more likely to use such awareness as a deterrent to anger build-up. If revenge were so sweet, we would be more inclined to support rather than sabotage one another, and be more of a mind to develop rather than do in our species.

TQ 45:   *"In my opinion what is 'I-can't-stand-it-itis' and what are its roots in anger control?"*

TA: "The term 'I can't stand it' encourages its believers to crank up their intolerance. It implies that what allegedly cannot be tolerated must be attacked. It is a vehicle for tensional build-up that must be expressed; after all, I can't stand not expressing such a strong feeling build-up."

RC: "I can't stand it" often is made to occur at three levels: (a) "I can't stand this bad occurrence (that has, is, or could happen)." (b) "I can't stand feeling so boggled about what I can't stand." (c) "I can't stand myself for not better managing circumstances and the feelings I create about them." "I can't stand it" is a statement of exaggeration, a dramatization of something that is unpleasant; but its discomforts are not beyond human tolerance.

TQ 46:   *"What do I believe the statement 'An eye for an eye and a tooth for a tooth - with a lot of blind, toothless people walking around' is meant to convey?"*

TA: "I think this statement communicates the folly of trying to get even; that no one wins in returning aggressive conduct preceded by anger."

RC: Revenge is an infantile daydream in that such roughhousing impacts negatively on everyone in the house. There are no winners with revenge fueled by anger. Anger's destructiveness takes no prisoners and does not consider its bombardment effects on all concerned.

TQ 47:   *"What do I conclude about the phrase 'If I hate the enemy, I become the enemy,' and how does it relate to the rudiments of anger?"*

TA: "I believe that this notion refers to angrily despising someone who has wronged you and then taking on features of your antagonizer, at minimum in a philosophical sense."

RC: When you hate someone who thwarts you, you adopt the worldview of that ruffian-behaving person. You may not do physical harm, but by your hate you prepare yourself to do so if you have the killing mentality in your craw. Hate is a four-letter word; multiplying it by two or more participants causes it to become all the more obscene.

TQ 48:   *"Who do I think is ultimately responsible for my angry feelings?"*

TA: "I am responsible for creating all my feelings including anger. More clearly put: others do not anger me, I anger myself about others' actions."

RC: It is not what you don't like that creates your anger, but your manner of thought, your words, your phrases, and your beliefs about what/whom you don't like that instigates anger. You trip your own emotional trigger by your language; reforming your self-language is the gateway to reforming your emotions.

TQ 49:   *"Which is the wiser view: 'They should know what I don't like and then honor my distaste' or 'It would*

> *be better for me to know by now that they are not about to honor what I wish not be done'?"*

TA: "I don't control others, and it would be better for me to conclude that they are going to continue to act according to their choices, not mine."

RC: Leaving margin for error, especially with others who consistently act badly, allows you to lower your expectations - as well as your pulse and heart rate. To expect others to follow their temperament, values, and disposition is to provide yourself emotional slack.

TQ 50: *"Do others have free-will? What is the tie-in of this hypothesis to anger?"*

TA: "Others have free-will to say, think, and do as they please; after all, I don't run the universe yet - though at times it may seem that I feverishly and foolishly am trying. My choice in matters of individual differences is whether I am going to hassle those who have the gall to think, feel, and act by their own sanctions.

RC: Avoiding notions that others are to have and hold values that are aligned to you, that "thou shalt have no other values apart from mine," and that others are entitled to your opinion and only your opinion is pure invented fiction - to be uninvented in the service of emotional well-being.

Each of the 50 questions posed in this chapter is part of a teaching, instructional method that permits readers to teach and instruct themselves about the multifaceted nature of anger. A practical understanding of anger's dimensions; profound, more tolerant philosophical changes; and forced anti-angry actions can result in making yourself into your own best anger-control counselor. Self-discovery of solutions is better than being spoon-fed answers by a third party. These 50 questions provide a comprehensive understanding of anger's anatomy. They take a hard look at the detailed mechanics of this goal-interfering emotion. Using these therapeutic questions to arouse your own therapeutic answers may turn out to be the best therapy you can get from anyone, anytime.

Note. From *You Can Control Your Anger! 21 Ways To Do It* by Bill Borcherdt. Copyright © 2000, Professional Resource Exchange, Inc., P.O. Box 15560, Sarasota, FL 34277-1560.

Chapter 6 Review Questions

1. Do you agree that others have the right to act badly toward you?

2. What does dissolving rather than expressing anger mean for you?

3. Why does anger expression increase rather than decrease anger?

4. How does undamning acceptance contribute to anger control?

5. What is the difference between angry and unangry restraint?

CHAPTER 7

"Who Does He Think He Is?"
Forgetfulness Dimensions of Anger

Anger has a short memory. Notice the first words often spoken in anger: "Who does he think he is?" (treating me this way; i.e., criticizing, ignoring, gossiping, disagreeing, accusing, etc.). This chapter will identify what the anger-ridden person typically forgets to do or not do. By smoking out what is ignored, ignorance is made ripe to be replaced with education, understanding, and information that can contribute to the awakening of logic and reason so as to dissolve anger before it dissolves you. How to halt yourself upon the brink of anger in time to remember to not forget what would be important to do or not to do to control this deadly emotion will be addressed. Specific practical suggestions will be given that invite and encourage you to pinch yourself so as to record in your mind what would be in your best interest to either remember or - in the case of matters relating to grudges, animosity, or resentment - to remember to forget to remember. Some reminders about the short memory that causes anger's short fuse include:

1. *Forgetting to selectively keep your yapper shut.* Forgetting to remain silent when under verbal fire lends itself to an-

gry escalation in that one is made into two people over-reacting to the other's unpleasantries.

2. *Not remembering to survey the big picture.* Is the world really coming to an end as you propose in your angry expressions? Perspective is a great quality, and it's important to understand how the presenting incident of concern fits into the overall scheme of things. That way you will not judge the whole by one or more bad parts.

3. *Failure to remember to not take disappointments personally.* Anger's efforts to control for better treatment from others reflects the insecurity one feels going without such favoritism. The more strenuous the effort to control the other, the greater the insecurity and the longer displeasure has been personalized. When you fail to remind yourself to not judge yourself by others' ill will, your personalizations will multiply your anger. After all, if I conclude that others' approvals are essential, and they fail to provide such necessity, then they are responsible for my misery - and are to be angrily condemned in a frantic, desperate effort to control for their provisions.

4. *Not recalling to not blame.* When you blame others for their shortcomings you are likely to produce anger toward them. If you blame yourself for your flaws in better coping with others' deficiencies, you build a case for anger at yourself.

5. *Forgetting to approach life nondefensively.* Remembering that you are not on trial and therefore aren't required to justify your existence, opinions, making requests, turning down requests, how you use your property, and how you spend your time frees you up emotionally because self-justifying pleadings often wash out into anger. This is because as you start to plead your case and to explain yourself, you are likely to overexplain in a hard-pressed way to gain others' presumed required understanding, ending up angrily putting yourself over a barrel due to your discov-

ery that no matter what you defensively say, it's not what the other wants to hear.

6. *Forgetting to not counterattack.* Remembering to avoid fighting fire with fire in not taking on the enemy's aggression sets health-saving boundaries on anger. Remembering not to beget another's anger with your own brand of intolerance helps keep a lid on the sum total of angry responses regarding individual differences. The less upset you counter(attack) with, the more emotional regulation is allowed to operate.

7. *Forgetting to admit that you, not another's words or deeds, however contrary they may be, are responsible for your angry feelings.* This puts you at the mercy of others who, in essence, have been given permission to pull your emotional strings. "I anger myself" will gain you better control over your life than "You got me angry." When you remember to address emotional accountability in this responsible manner, you will be less dependent on others to change before you can feel better.

8. *Forgetting to admit that you feel angry to begin with.* This leaves you without your foot in the door and not open to the possibility of changing your anger. Remembering the value of a philosophy of admittance over that of denial (i.e., "I am not angry!!") avoids the "little boy in big men's pants" or "little girl in a big girl's blouse" syndrome, wherein participants feel insecure about owning up to the facts of their anger disturbance.

9. *Forgetting that just because you have absolutistic ideas about how the world and people in it are to be does not mean that your values are almighty or even superior.*

10. *Forgetting that just because people are different from you does not mean you are better than they.* Evaluating differences can be educational; rating people by these differences generates anger.

11. *Forgetting not to feel sorry for yourself when you lose out on your taffy.* Self-pity when you don't get your own way is a step away from blaming others for your misfortune while angrily damning them in the process.
12. *Forgetting that anger represents emotional weakness, not strength.* A friendly reminder of the fear and insecurity behind anger's smokescreen can act as an encouragement to snuff it out.
13. *Forgetting to realize that you can't hurt someone else without hurting yourself.* This attitude will leave you leading the angry charge only to reveal its backfiring qualities.
14. *Forgetting to honestly and vividly call to mind where anger has brought you and the human species - on the edge of nuclear and missile warfare.* Such honest recall can prompt discouragement to express this evil, lethal emotion.
15. *Failing to remember to time project and put into perspective the long-range cosmic significance of what is being argued about, which in many cases is nil.*
16. *Forgetting to take a long-range view of anger's outcome by asking yourself, "Do I want to feel better right now by strongly releasing my anger, or do I want to feel better for the rest of my life by restraining myself and thusly avoiding angers backlashes?"* (i.e., loss of friends and opportunities).
17. *Forgetting to use four little words instead of four-letter words to describe the human condition: "Leave margin for error." Such permissive thinking permits a stifling of anger's uproar.*
18. *Forgetting to attribute what others' harsh conduct reveals about their mindset, instead judging yourself by their thinking about and conduct toward you.*
19. *Forgetting to remind yourself that some people will dislike you for the same reasons others warm up to you.*

20. *Forgetting to remind yourself that your efforts to express anger so as to get rid of it will fall on its face in that* the more you express anger the angrier you will get yourself.

Based on what can be learned from examining the forgetfulness dimensions of anger, the following tips are suggested to remember to manage - better yet, evaporate - anger in accordance with your long-range best interests.

- Adopt a philosophy of "Silence can be golden" and "The art of being wise is knowing what to overlook." Dispute less individual differences and others' lack of accommodation.
- Think holistically and don't judge life by one or a few bad omens or people in it.
- See that others' opinions do not equal you and that it is not a dire necessity that you win any popularity contests (though it may be nice if you did).
- Recognize that if you play the blame game you will be spitting fire and shooting anger in practically all directions. Blaming yourself, others, and/or life for your handicaps, faults, and deficiencies projects anger in whatever blaming direction you may have going for you at the time.
- Don't put your guard up. Be yourself rather than think that you are required to defensively prove yourself to your social group.
- Realize that fighting fire with fire will only result in your being burned longer and harder.
- Accept the fact that you trip your own emotional trigger and that your emotional enemy is - you!
- View admittance of the problem of angry disturbance as healthy and helpful; as a strength, not a weakness.
- Avoid arrogant thinking, where you view your opinions as all right and others' ideas as all wet.

- View individual differences as part of what makes life interesting, not something to be carped about.
- Boldly seek and remove any self-pity dimensions to your angry dilemmas.
- See that anger reads as vulnerability not invulnerability.
- Acknowledge that the main person you ordinarily end up hurting when you're angry is - you.
- Appreciate all the wrongdoings that have been done via anger so as to deter yourself from further contributing to such a rampaging mentality.
- See that in the long run much of what you anger yourself about has minimal lasting significance.
- Accept the present discomfort of anger pain for the long-range gains of anger restraint.
- Cut yourself some emotional slack by allowing for the human imperfection factor in otherwise strained relationships.
- Attribute others' poor behavior to be a reflection of their problems and disturbance and not a mirror of you.
- Remember to analyze the things others don't like about you as they sometimes reflect the very same things others will patronize you for.
- Admit that anger is an overreaction and the more you overreact the more skilled you make yourself at overreacting.

To remember to not forget the multiple problems and handicaps that anger creates can serve as an encouragement to not allow this crippling emotion to be on the loose. Anger stems from one-dimensional, demanding thinking. As a consequence, all the angry-feeling and angry-acting individual sees is red while readying to insistences and commands. "So, who does the angry-acting person think he is? Likely someone who deserves to get his own way because he is 100% right and others are 100% wrong. Better off he would be if he would instead remember and remind himself that he is someone who will sometimes get his own way and other times won't; in other words, to remember that he does not run the universe yet, though he may feverishly and foolishly be trying to do so. Locking this reality into his thinking will likely result in crowing less and making the most of things more often when matters of life do not stack up in his favor."

Note. From *You Can Control Your Anger! 21 Ways To Do It* by Bill Borcherdt. Copyright © 2000, Professional Resource Exchange, Inc., P.O. Box 15560, Sarasota, FL 34277-1560.

Chapter 7 Review Questions

1. How does anger encourage forgetfulness?

2. What do you think is the most important concept the angry-acting person fails to recall?

3. From this chapter content, what do you think is an especially good tip for extinguishing anger?

4. Do you believe that the more people overreact, the more likely they will become skilled in doing so?

5. How does attributing others' poor behavior as being a reflection of their problems help in better managing another's anger?

CHAPTER 8

Drunk Without Drinking:
Anger as an Intoxicating State of Mind

The appeal of something that feels good is more often than not allowed to override the question of whether it is good for you. Feel-good experiences are usually not debated as to their long-range feel-bad possibilities. The pleasure of the moment is set apart from any pain later on. Long-range negative consequences are literally pushed out of mind in favor of immediate pleasure. As a consequence, most anything that feels good is attached to a longing, a nostalgia to go back to it - and the devil be damned if it pains in the aftermath of the experience.

Partaking in angry indulgences is one of those "high" experiences that can leave you feeling low upon discovering what problems your rampages have created. Anger feelings and expressions provide a drug-free method of arriving at an intoxicated state that, though difficult to abstain from, is even more difficult not to. Anger's addictive qualities stem from the following cognitive and experiential factors:

1. *Emotional frenzy and fervor.* Angry-acting people are emotionally committed to their sacred values. They create a heightened state of emotionalism that goes unmatched in comparison to the often neutral state of mind that goes

along with neutral, everyday, routine experiences. High on their uppity feeling state, they hook themselves on their fervor and keep in mind for future reference this feverish emotional experience that is there for the angry asking.

2. *Creation of feelings of happiness.* The true believer may be happier than a skeptic, but this is no more significant than a drunk being happier than a sober person. People who challenge the belief system that creates their anger may seem to be less happy than those who get up on their high horse and proclaim rather than question their beliefs - and they may be, in the short run. However, in the long run they will likely bring more suffering upon themselves due to an unwillingness or an inability to consider better ways to live. The well may be left to run dry upon using up all the momentary slices of happiness.

3. *Self-righteousness.* Anger contains a fair amount of righteous indignation or "holier-than-thouism" that is often a cover up for "unworthier-than-allism." Nevertheless, believing not only that are your values superior but also that you are better than the next person and in the end of life will go up higher than others has its moments of emotional sparkle. Looking down upon others, which is intrinsic to anger, provides a drink without drinking feeling.

4. *Fanaticism.* Fanatics who angrily believe that "My way is *the* way" believe themselves to be deified for their angelic way of looking at things while others are to be angrily devilified. Fanaticism is practically always at the root of all emotional disturbance, whether the fanatical notion comes in the form of "should," "must," "have to," "got to," or "ought to." This bigoted approach to life reeks with insistences that promote an "in group" and an "out group," with a clashing of the wills to prove whose values are above the others.

5. *Keenness of mind illusions.* Anger fools its holders into believing that their thinking is sharper and keener when they are angrily drunk than when unangrily sober. In truth, an-

ger stems from demands that narrow, if not *eliminate,* the consideration of alternative methods of thought and conduct. Tunnel vision sets in, eliminating the possibility of compromise and cooperation. Thinking is dulled by anger in the long run, and a dull life is likely to transpire as individuals live out the one-and-only, pigeonholed script that they invented.

6. *Extremism.* Angry-behaving people tend to think in extremes, and the back and forth of it all can provide more than a little buzz in one's head. Extremists live on the edge, and it is that cutting edge that supplies increased adrenaline flow. Anger is made to set in when others disagree with the emotional charge and the frenzied message behind it.

7. *Heightened physiology.* Angry-acting people physically tighten up, that is, clench their teeth, tighten their fists, wrinkle their foreheads, and generally take on tensional mannerisms. When they eventually let go of their physical rigidity, a rush of relief ensues. It is this heightened feeling experienced in a physical context that has a return to attraction. Anger inflates, and it is the deflation that arouses calming feelings, only to have the anger-stress-relief cycle begin anew.

8. *Ego mania.* Humans tend to act like raving maniacs when they come across the opportunity to judge themselves as more worthwhile than someone else. Anger provides ego uplifting for those who think that they can use it. A little dab of anger toward someone who acts in disapproving ways can spark feelings of superiority that will hold your ego in check until the next pang of inferiority is felt - then back to the bottomless pit you will likely go in a futile attempt to use anger to support your own inferiority cause.

Intoxication, whether it be chemically or angrily induced, is a similar hearse with different license plates. Each in its own way results in blurred vision, ill-advised judgment, a strained relationship with life, and possibly deathly consequences. Golden rules are attempted to be made to exist when there are none. It takes a long time to find something that doesn't exist - including crisp, logical ideas when drunk, with or without drinking. So, sober yourself up in either case, detoxify yourself from anger and/or chemicals, lest you bring a toxic end to the one life that you will ever have.

Note. From *You Can Control Your Anger! 21 Ways To Do It* by Bill Borcherdt. Copyright © 2000, Professional Resource Exchange, Inc., P.O. Box 15560, Sarasota, FL 34277-1560.

Chapter 8 Review Questions

1. How can anger be considered to be fanaticism?

2. What is meant by the statement that because something is good it doesn't mean that it is good for you?

3. Why is anger a drunken state of mind?

4. How does anger fool people about their state of mind?

5. Why does anger eliminate a consideration of alternatives?

Life Without Taffy:
The Acid Test of Anger Control

This chapter will examine rational alternatives when getting your way is not forthcoming. Short of gnashing your teeth and angrily whining and screaming, there are more mature, civilized ways of anger control, even in the face of extreme adversity. It is like falling off a log to remain happy when the world and people in it seem to be bending our way. During these times of worldly accommodation it is easy to believe, at least weakly or once over lightly, that "I know I don't have to get my way all or any of the time." But when push comes to shove and the world and people in it reverse the bestowing of their advantages onto you and relinquish their adulation toward you, the acid test of anger control appears. In the moment of truth, when the incompatibilities between you and others hit the fan and your guardian angel goes on strike to boot, do you angrily pop off or poop out anger?

It's easier to make talking decisions than doing decisions. After all that is said and done there is more said than done, yet well done is better than well said. It is easy to talk in terms of tolerance, acceptance, grace, and forgiveness when not under siege from everyday annoyances and irritations - when matters of life are running as smooth as silk. Following is a list of cognitive and behavioral suggestions to consider when deprived of the taffy that your little heart desires. The cognitive suggestions begin with a rational debate that itemizes thoughts that create anger when frustrated, countered by thoughts that promote anger prevention. The items on the behavioral listing highlight the action component of anger control. These combined suggestions will assist in passing the acid test of anger control.

1. *Cognitive methods of anger control:*

    (a) *Rational debate.* List your common anger-producing self-statements and then debate; talk yourself out of them with separate countering rational conversations with yourself.

ANGER-PRODUCING IDEAS	COUNTERING ANGER-REDUCING IDEAS
• "It should be my time and turn to get what is owed me."	"The world runs randomly; there is no such taking-turns formula."
• "My good efforts must be returned."	"There are no logical reasons why I have to get a return on my investment."
• "I'm being especially pleasant so others must treat me accordingly."	"Others will treat me as they choose to, not how I choose them to."
• "I've gotten my taffy so far on this matter, so therefore I must continue to do so."	"Sometimes I will get my taffy and sometimes I won't; for the most part 'great' in the first instance and 'tough luck' in the second instance."
• "Others ought to do my bidding for me."	"I'm not (totally) helpless and can go to bat for myself."
• "When others say they are going to do something, they should deliver."	"As much as I would like others to be reliable, it does not mean that they must."
• "I must do exceptionally well and enjoy the sweet taste of success in my every endeavor."	"I hope to do well, but it is not essential that I do so at every turn."
• "My birthright is to do as I please and to be given what I want from life."	"I am in no way anointed, and in no way is the universe to give me strictly and only what I desire."

ANGER-PRODUCING IDEAS *(Cont'd)*	COUNTERING ANGER-REDUCING IDEAS *(Cont'd)*
• "People should appreciate me more than they do, and recognize me for the decent person that I am."	"People will draw their own conclusions about me. It would be wise for me to accept that some will put me in good standing while others won't."
• "Because I ask for so little taffy, I should get the small amount that I asked for."	"The world owes me nil, and the sooner I realize and accept that, the happier I will be."
• "I need and deserve a miracle."	"Happy people 'need' nothing nor do they believe in miracles."

(b) *Use holistic thinking.* View others, toward whom you have axes to grind, in a well-rounded way, including regularly thinking through those aspects of your relationship that are favorable, of benefit to you - lest you miss the boat of enjoying the part of the relationship that is enjoyable.

(c) *Use consequential thinking.* Fully consider the consequences of maintaining a prickly approach to your wounded-animal companion. What do you stand to lose in terms of present accrued advantages? What are the circumstances that anger could result in you being on the outside looking in? Where does your anger *really* get you?

(d) *Avoid finalistic thinking.* Statements that imply "This is the way he has been, is, and will continue to be" leave no room for the possibility for you to bend your thinking in the future. As a result, you will likely continue to make yourself eternally bent out of shape toward those you have written off as never possibly changing.

(e) *Stay away from overgeneralized thinking.* Believing that those who act badly are bad leaves you with a bad case of self- and/or other-condemnation.

(f) *Put the skids on catastrophic thinking.* Believing that something or somebody is "terrible," "awful," and/or "horrible" contributes to a snowballing of anger. As the description of what is undesirable is blown out of proportion, so too is anger escalated with such exaggerated means of expression.

(g) *Shake off fictional thinking.* Believing that someone or some circumstances "should," "must," or "ought not" exist when they really do is a pure invention that had best be uninvented so that reality as fact can be better accepted.

(h) *Set aside qualifying/hedging statements.* Don't hedge your bets by telling yourself "*Maybe* I'll forgive him," "I *guess* she has a right to be wrong," "I *might* learn how to better tolerate what I don't like," "*Possibly* there might be some truth to what he said," "I'll *probably* forgive her," or "I *could* work on my anger problem." All of these limp-handed commitments imply an out, a cop-out to be more precise, in that the dilly-dallying-speaking person can plead no contest by excusing inaction with "Well, I didn't say I would, I said I probably (might, could, possibly, maybe) would try to change my angry-acting ways."

(i) *Push away cause-effect, deterministic thinking.* Believing that circumstances that occurred just before your angry feeling caused your feeling leaves you with little bargaining power to assume responsibility for your emotions. As a result you allow yourself to be the plaything of your circumstances. "I embitter myself about circumstances rather than they anger me" is a more emotionally independent, hopeful, and accurate way of thinking.

(j) *Move away from personalized thinking.* Try to see that others' badly deficient conduct toward you does not represent you or them but rather their inability to live life more on the pleasant side. Look at their negative behavior not in anger, but in sorrow, regret, and compassion. The less personally you take others' ill-advised ways, the less anger you will create.

(k) *Give up sacrificial thinking.* If you live your life for others, putting them first and yourself a distant second, you will likely end up despising them. Instead, take on a philosophy of enlightened self-interest, putting yourself first and others a close second.

(l) *Abolish dictatorial, demanding thinking.* At the core of anger are insistences forced upon others who think different than the (true) believer. Without demands, anger could not begin its run against those who possess different values. Taking the sacredness (in the form of absolutistic demands) out of one's values will take the starch out of anger.

(m) *Avoid purposeful, oppositional thought.* Don't be a nagging dissenter and differ for the sake of differing. Such compulsive confrontation has a cumulative effect, resulting in a build-up of negative feelings in yourself and a wearing effect on others that is likely to convenience their own angry brand of fighting-fire-with-fire, oppositional behavior.

(n) *Dispel mandatory thinking.* Entering relationships with a philosophy of needing things from others encourages hostility and other-blaming (i.e., "It is essential that I gain certain provisions from you and when I don't cope well it's all your fault for not dispensing my requirements of you to me").

(o) *Engage yourself in long-range thinking.* Ask yourself: "Do I want to feel better right now by releasing my anger build-up, or do I want to feel better for the rest of my life by holding my angry horses while determining how I made myself angry to begin with?"

(p) *Put the skids on bigoted thinking.* All-or-nothing thoughts, where I am all right and you are all wrong, will endorse an angry build-up.

(q) *Propose individualistic, self-directed, and self-inspired thinking.* Seek the best way for you to look at matters of concern rather than how most people might angrily choose to do so. Don't put yourself through anger's hell in a handbasket just because a majority do.

(r) *Utilize situational-specific thinking.* Don't judge another by a simple wrongdoing - in fact, don't judge anyone! Don't evaluate a whole relationship by the sum of its parts. Don't overlap another's poor actions with the totality of your experiences with that person. This will help you to appreciate the good in the relationship while helping to neutralize hostile tendencies.

(s) *Incorporate empathic thinking.* Try to figure out the many reasons why your associate might be acting badly toward you; for example, perhaps he or she is unhappy if not miserable, or going through a difficult life or phase of life's adjustment. By walking a mile in the other person's moccasins you give tolerance an opportunity to put its walking shoes on en route to getting rid of animosity.

(t) *Generate more tolerant, flexible thinking.* Brainstorm the many, many ways there are to look at another's contrary conduct. Incorporating such attitude adjustments into your perspective gives you new, fresher, more rational ways of sizing up old, difficult problems.

(u) *Above all, learn to become your own best scientific thinker.* I think Albert Ellis's major contribution to peace and emotional well-being was his 1955 introduction of scientific thinking to the world community. Honestly challenge your anger-producing hypothesis. Ask and argue with yourself about the scientific evidence for what you believe to be true due to events that are followed by a build-up of anger. For instance:

- "Where is the evidence that those with whom I associate do not have a right to be wrong?"
- "Why must I be the one person in the universe who is not the recipient of others' thorny treatment?"
- "Where is it claimed that my values are sacred and therefore not to be betrayed?"
- "Where can it be verified that others must not purposefully thwart me?"
- "Can it be substantiated that my values are superior to others and that therefore I, Mr./Ms. Noble, am superior to them?"
- "How can it be proven that others can magically wiggle and squirm into my gut and give me a feeling of anger that they are then responsible for?"

2. *Behavioral methods of instilling anger control:* Defying, taking a stand against, and confronting faulty thinking has a way of loosening up frozen judgments that can then pave the way for behavioral tactics, such as those listed next, that prevent you from creating and escalating the ravishes of anger.

   (a) *Meet and greet the enemy.* Move toward those whom you are tempted to trip your own trigger about. In fact, act especially pleasant toward them. Taking on this philosophy of (unangry) nonavoidance provides you with a laboratory within which to practice and experiment with making yourself into a more tolerant human being.

(b) *Accommodate and add to the opportunity for your nemesis to act badly toward you.* Provide material such as mistakes you have made and things you have done that he or she would disapprove of. Here too you give yourself a chance to train yourself not to get yourself angry about another's barbs.

(c) *Stay active.* Do, don't stew. Don't obsess about others' unpleasant actions, as sitting on your hands only makes it convenient for you to repeatedly rake your displeasures over the coals, heating them up into anger.

(d) *Do behavioral rehearsals.* Ask a friend to challenge you to not anger yourself even when confronted with obnoxious accusations. Your friend can purposefully attempt to arouse your ire by taking on the harsh criticism of your adversary, giving you the chance to practice an unangry manner of approaching such seediness.

(e) *Write an essay.* Add to your understanding of the dual problem that anger can present by writing to yourself, "Why I don't have to get myself angry about anything, and why I don't have to put myself down if I do anger myself."

(f) *Utilize responsible self-expression.* Learn how to tell those who frustrate you how you feel without telling them off; for example: "I don't agree with what you just did and I want you to stop" versus "I hate what you did and I hate you."

(g) *Propose behavioral tradeoffs with the person you ordinarily make yourself angry about.* Suggesting that you and your adversary do things for each other rather than to each other can have an emotional melting effect.

(h) *Find some truth to what you generally disagree with in others and reflect it back to the person.* Highlighting commonality in what you largely disagree about can encourage more tenderness and less toughness as the relationship develops further.

(i) *Strongly agree with the other person even when you don't.* People like to be agreed with. By doing so you accommodate them which can help you to chisel away at your anger.

(j) *Show adulation for your opponent's enthusiasm.* Even if you totally disagree with the person you are in the habit of making yourself angry toward, tell him or her, "I admire the strength of your convictions" or "I can tell you have given your views a lot of thought." Such acknowledgments make it more difficult for all concerned to gain and maintain an angry stance.

(k) *Offer potentially workable compromises.* The very fact that you propose alternatives that would permit each of you to get at least part of what you desire can help produce a marshmallowing, softening effect that disinfects anger.

(l) *Ready yourself to use rejoiners rather than retaliators.* Having near the tip of your tongue (unangry) prepared statements can help to limit conflictual discussion and the anger that can piggyback off such verbal altercations.

Overall, blend in with the flow of another's attack rather than meet it head on, patronize another's view without compromising your own, act pleasantly even when you don't feel like it, and admit you're wrong even if you don't think you are. Such patronage influences others to cool their own emotions while allowing you behavioral practice sessions that prompt you to make yourself into a more tolerant, less demanding, and minimally angry-acting person. Anger is like acid that will destroy the container that holds it. Pass the acid test of anger control by passing on anger when you discover that the taffy you hoped for was not in the container that you expected.

Note. From *You Can Control Your Anger! 21 Ways To Do It* by Bill Borcherdt. Copyright © 2000, Professional Resource Exchange, Inc., P.O. Box 15560, Sarasota, FL 34277-1560.

Chapter 9 Review Questions

1. How is life without taffy - the acid test of anger control?

2. What is an example of an anger-producing idea in the fact of not getting your own way?

3. How can consequential thinking help reduce anger?

4. How does empathic thinking help to neutralize anger?

5. What do you think is meant by valuing blending in with the flow of the angry attack rather than meeting it head on?

CHAPTER 10

Extinguishing Anger Without Extinguishing Feelings

One irrational idea of what rational allegedly means is the assumption that if you get rid of anger you will then be without feelings. This false assumption discourages anger repentance for fear of becoming emotionally undressed. Rational thinking uses logic and reason in the service not the abandonment of your emotions. It helps you to feel more the way you want to feel and less the way you don't want to feel. One way to better service your emotions is to extinguish anger so that you can free yourself up emotionally to more freely choose other emotions that will better contribute to your long-range happiness and survival. Rational thinking is not a hard-shelled, mechanical method of thought that squelches all feelings so that the individual leads a drab, ho-hum emotional existence. Anger interferes with experiencing and expressing other, healthier emotions such as excitement, cheer, rejoicing, happiness, or exhilaration. This is because anger leads with a restrictive view that severely limits constructive emotional outgoingness. Rational thinking, on the other hand, puts forth a more permissive, expanded view that helps get you in tune with more fruitful feeling states that better contribute to your long-range best interests.

Novices who are trying to understand Rational Emotive Behavior Therapy, as well as some experienced practitioners who have some beginning familiarity with REBT, concern themselves needlessly about REBT's supposed unfeeling approach to human thought and emotion. They make themselves afraid of what they view as the possibility of having no emotional shadow to make themselves afraid of! Such worry is fit for a robot but not for a human being who practices rational thinking. Accompanying the fallacy that deficiencies of feeling are a consequence of thinking rationally are other groundless concerns such as that losing anger as a motivational tool will cause loss of motivation. On the contrary, letting loose of anger does not act as a disincentive. In fact, without anger, incentive becomes more productively harnessed. With anger the goal is to destroy; minus anger the goal is to produce. Anger reduction produces, not reduces, incentive and *appropriate* motivation, that is, motivation that results in less pain and more gain. Reduce anger - produce helpful results; produce anger - reduce healthy results.

Anger gets in the way of healthier living and can be reduced without fear that loss of anger will result in loss of feelings. Squashing anger without burying all, including more harmonious, feelings such as enjoyment, excitement, happiness, and exhilaration can be done by taking on philosophies of life (a belief system) that promote feeling expansion and emotional liberation. Following are some examples of: (a) thoughts that extinguish anger, (b) thoughts that arouse concern and annoyance that stop short of anger, and (c) other emotions that can be more freely expanded upon once anger is under wraps.

Thoughts that extinguish anger:

- "Others have a right to their faults."
- "It is not essential that life and others in it be kind to me."
- "My values are not superior as I sometimes make them out to be."

- "People are going to be the way they are and I need not hassle them about that."
- "It is near impossible to angrily harm others without harming myself."
- "Others have free-will and can willfully and freely trespass on my values."
- "Humans can (repeatedly) do the wrong thing."
- "Be sure to leave margin for error with others so as to prevent woeful disappointment."
- "I am not 100% right and he or she is not 100% wrong on any matter of dispute."
- "Others don't anger me, I anger myself by demanding that others have no other values before mine."
- "I am not special or anointed, and therefore others can frustrate me in any way that they choose to."

Thoughts that arouse protective emotions but stop short of anger, for example, displeasure, annoyance, irritation, disappointment, or distaste:

- "Let me set the record straight as to how disappointed I feel on this matter without telling him or her off."
- "I don't like being treated unkindly and will let those who do so know about my dislike, but that doesn't mean that they're required to honor my request for more gentle favor."
- "I don't like it when others betray my values, but because I don't like it doesn't mean it must not (frequently) occur."
- "I prefer a fairer shake on matters of attention, but I'd best not construe this preference to be essential to my overall happiness."
- "I like it when I am given even-handed consideration; in fact, I'll assertively seek it, but because I like it doesn't mean that I need it."

- "I hope to gain my social group's acceptance and approval, but as important as it is for me to do so, this positive recognition does not constitute my lifeline."
- "Because others may woefully misunderstand me does not necessitate a 'woe is me' response on my part."
- "It would be great to be acknowledged for the good works from my abundant efforts, and though it is disappointing when this does not occur, such a reality is far from being a monumental disaster."
- "It's fine to be appreciated, but when I displeasingly am not, this fact does not require me to define my ungrateful-acting associates as slugs."
- "I like it when others accommodate my heart and head's desires, and I find it irritating when they don't, especially if I use my time and effort to please them; but there is no universal mandate that says others have to do unto me as I kindly do unto them."

Feeling states that can be drawn from or more freely chosen once anger is kept down to a roar:

- Vigor
- Passion
- Love
- Kindness
- Excitement
- Enjoyment
- Exhilaration
- Fun
- Pleasantness
- Emotiveness
- Joy
- Creativity
- Happiness
- Peacefulness

- Accomplishment
- Satisfaction
- Contentfulness
- Eagerness
- Energetic
- Appreciation
- Confidence
- Decisiveness
- Harmony
- Gentleness
- Hopefulness
- Carefree
- Tenderness
- Sensualness

Rethinking your conclusions about matters of life creates a redoing of your emotions. Such attitude adjustments that come under the umbrella of accepting others' free-will rather than demanding that your will be loved, honored, and obeyed can reorder your emotions in a more tolerant, minimally angry direction. So, reshuffle your emotions by changing the thinking patterns that produce unhealthy emotions, such as anger. Do so without fear of becoming mechanized or "emotionless." Find out for yourself if extinguishing, killing anger does not bring more excitement and other feelings worth living for into your life. Unshackle yourself from anger and hang on to your hat for dear life as you ready yourself to experience slices of life and the attached feelings that you may not have known existed!

Chapter 10 Review Questions

1. Is a person required to give up feelings upon giving up anger?

2. What are some examples of healthy emotions that can be more conveniently experienced after anger is dissolved?

3. How is it that others have a right to their faults?

4. What feeling state would you most want to experience upon ridding yourself of anger?

5. Why are others not required to do unto you as you do unto them?

CHAPTER 11

Surveying the Wreckage:
Avoiding the Hazards of Fixing
Another's Wagon

"I'll fix his wagon" is the often-heard threat of someone who believes another has instigated against his best interest and voices his intent to do harm to this person. This battle cry reflects the "eye for an eye, tooth for a tooth" mentality that often results in a lot of broken teeth and one-eyed people walking around. Vengeance has its backlash, retaliatory complications, and consequences that create further relationship breakage. What the wagon-fixer fails to realize is the long-range dangers of angry admonishments set in motion. Angry focus is often put on the immediate, feel-good, expressional appeal of it to the neglect of the aftermath debris. Wrecking another's wagon by "fixing" it is a paradox that spells danger, harm, and often indefinite relationship difficulties. Fixing (wrecking) another's wagon can wreck relationships and sabotage other areas of living as well.

Some will cling to their rightful and self-righteous angry capacities while maintaining that "anger is not bad, its what you do with it that's dangerous." These famous last words fail to take one minute to consider the dreadful things that humans have done when anger is released unharnessed, as it practically always is. As its intensity builds, it begins to snowball, running roughshod over anyone and everything that gets in its way. This chapter will survey the emotional wreckage often found to be the cause of get-even intentions. What follows is a list of anger-related feeling possibilities that are made to occur as motivation to do the other in, to "fix his/her wagon." Such reflection can help to paint a portrait of "What am I really doing when I anger myself?" "Where does it really get me?" and "What would be a better way to look at and to manage my dislikes beyond trying to harm someone?" Earmarking others for harm is created by the following emotional disturbances, all of which are similar to and fall under the umbrella of anger:

1. *Resentment.* This silent expressing of anger creates harmful distance between people that is often irreparable.
2. *Bitterness.* This branch of anger is nearer the surface than resentment and is often accompanied by self-pity and sulking.
3. *Animosity.* This portable form of anger keeps your nose stuck up in the air as a silent expression of anger. As with some of the compartments of anger, a picture is worth a thousand words.
4. *Aggression.* This dramatic venture springs from anger with leaps and bounds, building wildfire momentum that is difficult to put out. This is the main risk of anger; eventually it is often targeted toward a person, place, or thing that one has made oneself angry toward.
5. *Hostility.* To spit fire readies one for angry release, and this is what this anger section does.
6. *Vindictiveness.* This state of mind represents a chunk of anger that is ready, willing, and capable of busting loose in an aggressive direction.
7. *Vengeance.* Plotting and scheming to do unto others as you perceive them as having done unto you are steady trademarks of this not so steady angry game plan.

8. *Retaliation.* This action component follows the development of a road map to cook another's goose.
9. *Spite.* Perhaps the most quiet of the angry feeling states is this ever-ready emotion. Spite serves as a power enhancer in that while putting yourself in the throes of spite you can think as viciously as you choose to about another, and they can't do a thing to stop such an internal barrage.
10. *Unforgiveness.* Forgiveness melts anger, unforgiveness hardens it. Unforgiveness leaves Pandora's box open so that anger with all its aspects can partake in its war games.
11. *Sulking.* Passive-aggression demonstrates yet another, silently hardened manner of expressing dislike and disdain.
12. *Hate.* This four-letter word makes anger regulation near impossible due to the fanatic philosophies that support it.
13. *Viciousness.* The intensity of this feeling serves the purpose of getting ready to strike out toward others who have the nerve to defy your deified values.
14. *Rage.* Another four-letter word that gives vent to anger as obscenity.
15. *Fury.* Step in step with rage, this top-of-the-line angry sentiment can create utter destruction between life's elements.

These are the offshoots of anger that are used when you take it upon yourself to be the judge and jury in the reprimand and punishment of those who have slighted you. So that you don't get yourself caught up in these same potholes of anger you can learn from rather than repeat others' overreaction. This can be done by reminding yourself of rational ideas that keep each of these barriers to peace and harmony under wraps. Each of the 15 relatives of anger listed is followed by:

(a) the irrational belief that propels the destructive emotion (IB) and
(b) a rational belief that conveys a more tolerant, accepting view designed to buffer anger and its derivatives before they get off the ground (RB).

1.   *Resentment*

IB: "How dare anyone treat me so dastardly. I'll remember this shoddy treatment until the day she dies - and I hope it's soon."

RB: "How foolish that I cling to my ill-willed feelings about another's ill-advised treatment of me."

2.   *Bitterness*

IB: "Let me show him just how strongly I can hold a grudge; that way he will feel both guilty for harming me and worried about when I might counterattack his wickedness."

RB: "Who am I really harming when I embitter myself unceasingly? While I am torturing myself for others' wrongdoings, they are out having a blast (while I sit home and sulk)."

3.   *Animosity*

IB: "The more ill-willed that I make myself feel, the more this shows the world what a strong-willed person I am. Clinging to my harsh feelings is a declaration of strength."

RB: "Stop kidding yourself. The more animosity I cling to, the more of an emotional mouse I represent and the bigger emotional baby who clings to his security blanket I cause myself to be."

4.   *Aggression*

IB: "I must show the world and others in it how angry I am or else they will think they can always take advantage of namby-pamby, little bitty old me."

RB: "Dramatically addressing my anger will only get me into personal, interpersonal, legal, employment, and health problems - to name a few. The only thing that this will be a clear demonstration of is my deficiencies in not taking disappointing circumstances and making them worse."

5. *Hostility*

IB: "I'll seethe not soothe my wounds, because that will better ready me for the field of battle, if it comes to that, which it likely will."

RB: "Better that I ready myself to do battle with my stubbornness and pigheadedness to resist forgiveness of others than to embellish them with hostility and entice them to do battle, and beget my anger."

6. *Vindictiveness*

IB: "If I don't remain at the cutting edge of angry action I might find myself a victim of a sneak attack by my oppressor."

RB: "Better that I vindicate than be vindictive, that way I will be less hair triggered when others approach me in an unpleasant fashion."

7. *Vengeance*

IB: "I'll get even for every knock that he has given me - and then some. If I don't get my sweet revenge he will think that he can walk all over me whenever he pleases."

RB: "Acts of vengeance will only boomerang on me, and what I once believed to be sweet washes into sourness as my vile acts inevitably come back to haunt me. Vengeance also results in me automatically taking on the revenge of my opponent as a childhood daydream, rather than think of other anger-coping options."

8. *Retaliation*

IB: "Tit for tat with no questions asked. I'll borrow a page from her anger book and identify exactly how she treated me and return the disfavor precisely as it was turned toward me."

RB: "Retaliation is like fool's gold, what you dramatically see is not what you get. Retaliation appears that you are evening up the score when in reality you are contributing to the displeasure of an already wounded animal while encouraging others to treat you poorly even more often."

9.   *Spite*

IB: "How good it feels to spite others who are not on the same page that I am. I can think as badly about them as I so choose - and they can't do a thing about it; weak them, powerful me!"

RB: "Spite saps time and energy, commodities that I don't have an indefinite amount of; better that I put what resources I do have to use in ways that will assist me in feeling more the way I want to feel and less the way I don't want to feel - and spite is disqualified as an aid for that purpose."

10.   *Unforgiveness*

IB: "I'll be dipped if I'll spend the least bit of time and effort overlooking to say nothing about forgiving others for all their trespasses too numerous to mention. If I forgive them this will just give them an excuse to continue to go against me."

RB: "How do I want to live? With a chip spiked on to my unforgiving shoulder or more with a marshmallow in my mouth? Forgiveness would seem to have more safe, pleasant appeal than harder, unpleasant false pride that blocks me forgiving others."

11.   *Sulking*

IB: "By grudgingly pulling into my self I'll punish others who will feel guilty for being a contributor to my misfortune. These same associates will feel sorry for me when they openly view me as purposefully presenting myself as the statue of misery."

RB: "What a waste! All sulking does is give me ample opportunity to practice 2-year-oldism, silently whining like the little baby who cannot have her candy."

12.   *Hate*

IB: "The more I hate another the bolder I can allow myself to think, feel, and act in nonconstructive angry ways."

RB: "The fanaticism and fervor that reflect hate are exceptionally difficult to control, better that I watch my step lest I get to a point of no emotional return. If I act on my hate there is no telling what my capacity to harm others might be."

13.   *Viciousness*

IB: "OK, if he wants to go to opposite corners I'll come out swinging like he has never seen anyone coming out swinging before."

RB: "Is utter destructiveness really the way I want to live in this life that does not feature a dress rehearsal? This is not the preliminary, this is the main event, and I would do well to put more into the peace process than the war games."

14.   *Rage*

IB: "I just can't help myself when I get myself angrily revved up. You will just have to excuse me for being at the mercy of getting myself so caught up in this tunneled-vision emotion where all I can see is red."

RB: "I would do well by taking more responsibility for the building and expressing of this nuclear emotion, because until I do it is unlikely that I will be able to better control it. I can do this in advance of a problematic situation by practicing strongly reminding myself that

I trip my own trigger while rehearsing in my head a more mannerly emotional and behavioral response to what I don't like."

15.   *Fury*
IB: "The more I let fury fly the more intimidated others will make themselves, giving me a decided advantage in the race for what I consider right. What better method of control than letting fury rain so as to bolster my chances of getting my own way?"
RB: "Furiously controlling for getting my own way simply begets more fury from others, lending to explosive possibilities."

Mending differences is better than bending the truth to fit your irrational angry hypothesis. Attempts to fix another's wagon only break it further. Fix your thoughts rather than make yourself angrily fixated on them. That way you won't give yourself an angry breakdown and will have no wreckage to survey.

Note. From *You Can Control Your Anger! 21 Ways To Do It* by Bill Borcherdt. Copyright © 2000, Professional Resource Exchange, Inc., P.O. Box 15560, Sarasota, FL 34277-1560.

Chapter 11 Review Questions

1. How does figuratively fixing another's wagon actually poison relationships?

2. What is risky about the position statement that "anger is not bad, it's what you do with it that's dangerous"?

3. What do you think is the most common form of emotional disturbance of those discussed in this chapter that earmarks others for harm?

4. Why is it irrational to refuse to forgive others for their trespasses?

5. What would be a good rational belief that would counter feelings of hostility toward another?

CHAPTER 12

Unangrily Putting Your Foot Down
Without Overstepping Your Bounds

Setting limits on your relationships with others can be a
life and relationship saver. It can also provoke life and relationship problems if done angrily, without discretion or consideration for the manner, style, and motivations for you to draw a
line in the sand. To be action oriented in firmly protecting yourself from others' unrealistic expectations and unfair advances
is vital to your self-interests and mental health. In setting boundaries for what you will tolerate and do in your interpersonal
relationships, consider that it is not simply what you say in
carrying out your boundary limitation message, but how you
make yourself feel and appear while you do it. Also, and for the
purposes of this chapter, the reasons for your limit-setting on
anger is what constitutes whether you are overstepping the
bounds of rational civilized thought, emotion, and behavior.
This chapter will consist of four parts:

Part I   Examine and fine tune thoughts that result in angrily
overstepping logic and reason while running rough-
shod against others who seem to be trying to take
advantage of you.

Part II   Quelling thoughts that bring your feelings into more rational focus so as not to push yourself too far in getting your limit-setting objectives to be clearly understood.

Part III   General characteristics that are a tip-off to your angrily overstepping the firm limitations you wish to apply.

Part IV   A review of the advantages to preferably rather than demandingly address your concerns.

Part I

Thoughts that cause anger and aggressively overstep your bounds. To make a fine-tuned determination as to whether you are going perhaps as far as you have ever gone with a no-nonsense, limit-setting assertion or too far in a reckless, aggressive direction, examine your ideas that created the emotion that propelled your behavior in your boundary-setting endeavor. Ideas that hasten anger with the frequent result of an aggressive overkill created as seen in the cloud of dust as you stomp off include:

- "I hate him and I'll demonstrate just how much!"
- "I'll show her who is boss!"
- "I'll put my foot down and trample all over him while I'm at it!"
- "I'll rudely give her a dose of her own medicine!"
- "I'll call upon myself to be the authority around here!"
- "I'll get the upper hand, regardless of cost!"
- "I'll make sure he wished like hell he had never pushed me to this point!"
- "She put her foot in her mouth once too often; this time I'll shoot it while it's there!"

- "I'll give him a lesson in humility that he wished he had never learned!"
- "I'll remind her that she has gone too far for my blood, even if it means bloodying her!"
- "I have to multiply my desires to get my point across or else he will think I'm afraid of him and don't really mean business!"
- "Who does she think she is - Queen Elizabeth or someone - I'll dethrone her in a quick hurry!"
- "It will take a minor miracle for him to live through what punishment I am about to bestow on him for asking too much of me!"

Part II

Quelling, self-disciplined thoughts that better allow you to tell others how you feel without telling them off:

- "Express, don't explode!"
- "Set limits, not hurt lives."
- "Self-interest is nice, overkill is not necessary!"
- "Tell others how you feel, don't tell them off!"
- "Stay concerned, don't let yourself get consumed!"
- "Involve yourself in your concerns, don't entangle yourself in them!"
- "Don't pour it on too thick!"
- "Preferably give alternatives rather than ultimatums!"
- "Put your best foot forward rather than use it as a swift kick."
- "Examine your intentions."
- "Hold fire!"
- "Get yourself fired up - but not too hot!"

Part III

Characteristics that tip off that aggressiveness is winning out over assertiveness:

1. *Hostile voice tone.* Verbal attack not only comes in the form of what you say but also the gruff yelling and screaming with which you say it.
2. *Angry, disapproving facial features.* Frowns, grimaces, and glares often reflect the anger behind the message.
3. *Physical gestures.* Clenching of fists, finger pointing, and stomping of feet often reflect anger that has gone beyond simple forthright limit setting.
4. *Excessive physical closeness.* Extending yourself nose to nose as you dramatically drive home a message suggests a not so underlying angry-feeling state.
5. *Mocking and mimicking.* Taking on the other's manner and demeanor in excessive portions is a needling method of communicating anger.
6. *Sarcastic reflection.* Angrily exaggerating what you view as the other's errors carries anger expressed in this heightened manner.
7. *Use of pet nicknames.* Hitting below the belt by addressing your associate with nicknames he or she has been known not to appreciate, for example, "Hey shorty," "Now listen, fat boy," "Watch yourself, four eyes," "I've got something to say to you, peg leg," all reflect anger beginning to simmer.
8. *Purposeful interruptive behavior.* Intentionally interrupting the other as he or she attempts to respond to your accusation is part of what leads you down the (angry) garden path.
9. *Overexplaining and oversimplifying what you have to complain about in an effort to "insult the other's intelligence" represents another calculated effort to express an-*

ger. Attempting to put another in a one-down position by addressing your associate as if he or she was a child can be a sly way of expressing anger.
10. *Grave digging.* Listing not only the current complaint but all past grievances lends itself to anger build-up at each level of description.

Part IV

Advantages of setting limits but not taking yourself to or over the angry limit.

Restraint is an exceptionally important ingredient of relationship lubrication. Without this unique form of patience, relationships will remain strained if not severed. Yet, before one makes a change from overstepping to stepping out of one's bounds, it is likely they will require to foresee, if not figuratively smell, the advantages of doing so. This is simply part of a general human condition reality; that there are few people on this green earth who will modify their approach to others until they have a keen sense that there is something in it for them. Advantages of a firm, respectful, yet forthright, no-nonsense approach to putting your foot down without overdoing the matter include:

1. *Likelihood of gaining and sustaining the other's attention, now and in future encounters, is increased.* Openly making bold statements about matters of concern to those who account for them keeps them more attentive to your messages.
2. *Prevents you from wearing yourself out by trying to accommodate others at nearly every turn.* Anger and resentment are prevented when you put yourself first and others a close second. By not bending or sacrificing yourself to a fault you don't allow yourself to exclusively sacrifice

yourself for others so as to end up despising those you
have given too freely to.

3. *May increase respect from others.* Those who observe you
sensibly and civilly setting boundaries may admire your
emotionally healthy approach.

4. *Increases your own meaning and appreciation for life.* Putting your best foot forward on your own behalf signifies
that you believe that there are important things in life that
you think are valuable enough to be in search of.

5. *Allows you to practice accepting yourself.* When you set
boundaries you risk others' disapproval, which then provides you with the opportunity to become familiar with the
value of accepting yourself even when others don't.

6. *Liable to sleep better and feel less stress and tension as
you begin to take more control over your life.* Life is better
organized when you and others know what to expect from
one another.

7. *More practical advantages.* As you emotionally free yourself up by setting the record straight in terms of what you
will put up with and what you will not put up with you are
in a better position to focus on striving for what you want,
refusing to accept what you don't want, and, as a consequence, likely to land your goals more often.

8. *Life is made into a two-way street with more give and take,
rotation, and balance between you and your peers.* Everybody gets a more complete piece of the pie rather than
somebody ending up with a few crumbs.

9. *Elimination of blank checks resulting in the elimination of
others taking advantage of you.* As you address the issue
of your no longer being willing to give with no expectation in return, you will likely experience betrayal less frequently.

10. *More hope being generated.* As you shake off compulsive
compliance trappings, hope at the end of the tunnel can be
seen more clearly.

11. *Develops expressional skill training that may generalize to other social circumstances.* As you ask bold questions and make bold statements in one social sector such capacity may be transferred to another circumstance.
12. *Self-encouragement is put into practice.* Pushing and encouraging yourself to say what is on your mind in a manner that is in your best interest to do so is a good habit to get yourself into.
13. *Increases capacity for tolerance.* Moving away from intolerant, angry-producing ideas, for example, "I can't stand what he has done and I'll tell him off like he has never been told off before and like I have never told anyone off" to "I'll tell her how I feel without telling her off," creates more patience and restraint than you thought you had.
14. *Increases performance confidence.* As you begin to see yourself as a person who can successfully do on his or her own behalf you will be more likely to take risks, attempting to say and do things you once feared saying and doing.
15. *Less ill will toward others.* When you begin to run your own life better, you are likely to put animosity on the run, rather than angrily thinking you are boxed in due to others' requests, expectations, and taking you for granted.

When you put your best foot down without overstepping your bounds, you are less likely to get this same foot stepped on. As a result you will be more likely to know and experience fewer of life's boundaries, bumps, and bruises and more of its up side rather than its down side. Maintaining boundaries makes for a more bountiful existence!

Chapter 12 Review Questions

1.   What are some typical thoughts that create anger?

2.   What do you think are the three main tip-offs to anger?

3.   Is it more effective to set no-nonsense limits when angry or when not experiencing anger as a feeling state?

4.   What do you think is the main advantage of a direct yet unangry approach to relationships?

5.   What do you think is the main disadvantage of angrily trying to set the record straight?

CHAPTER 13

Double Dipping Anger:
How Sweet It Is Not

Rational Emotive Behavior Therapy teaches clients how to not emotionally disturb themselves for having problems, and that if they do blame themselves for their faults, such reprimands are likely part of a more comprehensive problem of self-downing. It then goes on to teach consumers how to unconditionally accept themselves with their problems, holding that until a foundation of self-acceptance is in place, the problem-solving progress will not begin. Accepting yourself with no external props can emotionally free you up to more clearheadedly manage the practical and emotional problems that exist in life. Double dipping may taste sweet when savoring ice cream, but when resolving emotional and behavioral problems the sweetness is lost as double dipping becomes double whammy.

Double dipping is turned into double whammy when people overreact, angering themselves about a frustrating circumstance in life and continuing forth with their anger, venting it toward themselves for their emotional slippage. Anger is double dipped by the use of the following derogatory self-statements:

- "What an ass I am for acting assininely."
- "How stupid I am for stupidly blowing my top."

- "What a fool I am for bringing on this angry foolishness."
- "You idiot!"
- "What a numbskull I must be for blowing my cool."
- "What a worm I turn into for flipping my wig."
- "What a bad, evil, vile, putrid human being I am for conducting myself so horribly."
- "I must only do splendid things and never do bad things to consider myself to be anything other than subhuman."

Far better it would be to lighten up on yourself, to leave margin for error, and to understand that compassion begins at home. That way anger could be corralled at level one rather than you stepping in number two by doubling up on this hardened emotion. You could more ably concentrate on overreacting less in the future than dividing your energies up by condemning yourself in the present. The commonly held problem-solving myth is that to tend correctively to your problems you must first whip yourself for having them. The truth is that such double dipping is unnecessary and blocks the likelihood of discovering remedies to what ails you. To get beyond double dipping, double whammy, where you give yourself a self-blame problem about the original problem, install the following compassionate self-statements in your everyday value system:

- "Get after your behavior without getting after yourself."
- "Get after the act but not the actor."
- "Reprimand your conduct without whipping yourself."
- "Find fault but not blame."
- "I do my errors but I am not my blunders."
- "Give yourself some emotional slack."
- "I'm human, not subhuman, and to think otherwise would be 'inhumane.'"
- "Do the correction, don't re-do the mistake."
- "Correction, certainly! Condemnation, most certainly not."

- "Down with the mistake without down with myself."
- "I am not a blundering idiot for idiotically blundering."

Little in life is sweeter than accepting yourself unconditionally as you are. Little is more bitter than the cumulative effect of giving yourself a report card with a bad mark when your faults and deficiencies rear their ugly heads. Due to your remarkable imperfect nature you will on occasion, perhaps on many occasions, anger yourself toward life or others in it. It is at that point you will be required to decide whether to double dip, to get yourself a second scoop of anger, this one at yourself for making yourself angry, or to focus more on problem correction. As you are determining how to respond, try to remember that not only do two wrongs not make a right, but two brands of anger are less manageable and less in your best interest than one. That way you will be more likely to avoid a double dose of anger in all its sweetness that it is not.

Chapter 13 Review Questions

1.   What is double whammy?

2.   How does Rational Emotive Behavior Therapy teach how not to emotionally disturb oneself for having problems?

3.   What are some thoughts that avoid self-blame?

4.   What does "give yourself some emotional slack" mean for you?

5.   What does unconditional self-acceptance mean for you?

CHAPTER 14

Defending To Your Death Anyone's Right To Agree With You: Fundamentals of (Un)Angry Disagreement

It seems much simpler to defend another's opinion and his or her right to voice it when it happens to be one that we share. Such built-in compatibility is convenient in successful relationships. It's just easier to associate with others when they patronize our values. Truth is often a convenience item, and when others see things similar to the way we do, well, two geniuses can't be wrong now, can they?

Problems arise when others disagree before they learn how to agree to disagree. This is like playing baseball in the major leagues before you learn the rules and rudiments of the game. The rules of learning how to defend others' right not only to agree with you but also to disagree with you include:

1. *A decent respect for individual differences.* The more you learn to appreciate that each person you meet is an experiment of one, the less angry you will make yourself when you don't see eye to eye with someone.
2. *Leaving margin for error.* These four words, when applied, make it easier to forgive others for, rather than fight them because of, their mistakes.

3. *Accepting the reality of free-will.* Understanding that others have free-will and not your will prevents harboring ill will toward them.

4. *The right to be wrong.* Digesting the grim reality of others' right to error especially strengthens the gut on the way down when it is applied not only to people generally but to those with whom you associate on a daily basis. It is often easier to take on a liberal view when your opinion concerns those that you view from afar, while those who are located underfoot cannot cut muster by way of their rights to be wrong. Here is an example of one person questioning another on the topic and the typical responses:

Question #1:   "Do you believe others have a right to be wrong?"

Answer #1:   "Why most certainly I believe that others have a right to be wrong!"

Question #2:   "How about *this* person with whom you associate on a daily basis; does he/she have a right to be wrong?"

Answer #2:   "Are you kidding? The people and especially *the* person whom I deem as being most significant in my life have absolutely no right to be wrong (toward me) because I should be the one person in the universe to have and to hold on to someone who is without fault and disturbance."

How quickly one can make oneself go from liberal to conservative when the social context is considered. The closer to home the mistake is made, the more difficult it is to accept and forgive.

5. *Giving yourself high frustration tolerance (HFT) rather than low frustration tolerance (LFT).* Make yourself more

tolerable of others' disagreements with you by saying to yourself, "I can stand it when others disagree with me and would do well to expect that they will often do so."

6. *Understanding and accepting human variability.* Humans are ever changing and with their ongoing changes will sometimes begin to disagree with you about matters of previous compatibility. "He turned on me" is the battle cry of the person who has not learned and accepted that people will change their values and what was once of shared importance is no more. To realize that people have equally as much right to their divergent views as to their accommodating views is a test of a mature, civilized life's perspective.

7. *Realizing that when others disagree with you they are not against you but for their own values.* Tucking away this information and pulling it out when tempted to anger yourself can administer neutralizing if not dissolving effects when tempted to personalize another's perspective that happens to be in contrast to yours. Unlearning the paranoiac belief that others' dissident ideas are attempts to do you in can salvage relationships.

8. *Letting well enough alone.* So what if others acquire and practice a perspective that cleans its slate of your ways of looking at things. As long as these are not attempted to be force-fed to you, what difference does it make? What really matters is you know what you stand for, and if others sponsor other values rather than patronize yours, so be it. Even when conversing with those who obviously feel strongly about what they believe in which is what you don't subscribe to - for example, topics such as religion, assisted suicide for the infirm, politics, economics, raising children - you can patronize these distinctions rather than anger yourself about them by simply (unangrily) nodding your head to signify understanding while letting the distinctions settle rather than meddle into the conversation.

9. *Approach relationships with ideas of parity.* Realizing that we are all in life together and no one is better than anyone else lends itself to realizing that just as no one is superior, so too are one's values not necessarily superior. As a result, there will likely be less feuds and more hearing out of alternative notions which washes out to more mutual understanding of and learning from one another.

10. *Developing the capacity to give with virtually no expectation in return includes giving your opinions and having them frowned upon.* This is a litmus test of accepting others' right to disagree with you; putting your best opinion forward, getting it stepped on - and not catastrophizing about it.

11. *Appreciating human fallibility.* Humans err in everything they do, including judgments that form the basis for their values. They often make position statements with rigid, inflexible, unscientific thinking patterns. To accept others' narrow-minded and short-sighted disagreements as being due to their remarkable fallible nature can prevent wars and rumors of wars between you and others who perhaps out of ignorance have the gall to defect from your values.

12. *Emphasis on interdependence.* We have a practical dependency on one another to supply those goods and services that could otherwise not be gained. Just as we use each other to accumulate practical resources, so too can we use each other to learn new ideas from each other - that is, unless we fight only for the right of others to see life through our peepers - and ours only!

13. *Undo allergies for preference.* Emotional disturbance has its origins in preferences (what you want), but humans are quick to make themselves allergic to preferences and multiply them into demands (what you think you need). The following illustrates how escalating preferences cause anger:

Rational
Preferential Idea: "I prefer, want, wish, desire that my associate either agree with me or agree to disagree with me." (Resultant feeling of irritation, annoyance, displeasure, and disappointment when preferences reached for are not gained.)

Irrational
Demand Idea: "Because I prefer that others agree rather than argue with me, they absolutely and most assuredly have to/ must/should/have got to/ought to." (Feelings of anger, hostility, resentment, hostility, rage, and fury when demands for agreement are not captured.)

14. *Ingraining an attitude of forgiveness.* Forgiving others because they have a different view of the world than you while defending their right to do so fosters (un)angry disagreement.

15. *Plant a respect for human limitations.* Humans are limited in their capability to understand and to agree with one another. Incompatibility is a given of the relationship of any two people. This is simply because all people are different, but it is only when these differences are not accommodated and instead argued about that boundary disputes occur.

16. *Accept that it's difficult to get any two people to agree on anything.* Humans have their own agendas and will follow their own noses, often ending up in opposite directions than you. Accepting rather than overreacting to or personalizing this reality is an important ingredient of anger control.

17. *Recognize and accept that nothing between any two people is ideal - far from it - but less than ideal isn't required to mean no good - far from it.* You can still enjoy those parts of the association that are in sync.

18. *Appreciate the comforting reality that you will likely learn more from those who disagree with you.* Talking with those whom you agree with makes for another day at the office, while conversing with the loyal opposition makes available opposing views that can contribute to a more well-rounded life experience. A sure way to corrupt your mind is to hold in lower regard those who think differently than you. Be glad for opposing views, for they help you to more keenly stay on your toes.

19. *Unveil human contradiction and don't allow it to throw you for a loop.* Humans will say one agreeing thing on a given matter one time and a disagreeing thing on the same matter another time. This frustrating inconsistency cannot be made to fuel longer by protesting against it.

20. *Dig in your heels in favor of human rights to be odd, unusual, and peculiar - more than different.* The bigger the gap in viewpoints, the stranger sounding others opinions are, or the more unconventional another's position, the more likely and stronger will the fire of the disagreement be fanned rather than doused. Even though new ideas are more likely to flourish in a climate of unconventionality, the greater the size of the difference in opinion the stronger the insistence on agreement is likely to be made.

21. *Establish anticatastrophizing, deawfulizing, and squelching of exaggerating descriptive explanations.* Because others may not view what is truth as you view it does not constitute a calamity. Disagreement is not disaster unless you let it be so. Settle yourself down about your disagreements and you will more likely make a settlement about them.

22. *Cultivate some more philosophies of tolerance and acceptance.* Train yourself to agree to disagree - but not

too strongly. The more you are able to give yourself heavy doses of tolerance about and acceptance of diverse views, the more clearheaded you will be able to approach your differences with others in a collaborative, cooperative, compromising, and unangry way. When you seek others' opinions try to do it with a no-strings-attached approach.

Avoid the implication that suggests others ask, "Do you want me to say what I want to say or what I think you want me to say?" Call your own bluff and honestly ask yourself if you want to hear of ideas that are different from yours. Self-sentences that purify and help preserve the grievance, disagreeing process include:

- "Best that I learn to better tolerate the charge of others' disagreements; otherwise I will encourage them to only say things that they think will meet with my approval and then I will not get to know them on an honest basis."
- "If I don't develop the emotional endurance necessary to deflect and deal with disagreement, life will be a long row to hoe in that any two humans are different in some fashion."
- "Avoid 'Say what I want to hear' and embrace 'Say what is on your mind and I promise not to throw cold water on whatever that might be.'"
- "(Un)angry, honest disagreement is usually better than dishonest agreement."
- "Often it is far better to have tried to encourage others to be forthright with me and fail to gain their agreement than it is for them to beat around the bush of disagreement in a frantic effort to get me to like them."
- "Relationships that can't stand the test of controversy are unlikely to stand the test of time."
- "Agreeing to disagree opens up new areas of learning, while agreeing to agree blocks knowledge possibilities."

- "Best that I encourage others to exercise their rights to state their views, so when it comes time to state mine I will be more likely to get a listening ear from others."
- "Open-mindedness expands life's opportunities, closed-mindedness diminishes life's quality."
- "A 'Be reasonable, see it my way' philosophy makes for unreasonable expectations and outcomes."
- "In the interest of democracy, better that I defend others' rights to agree *and* to disagree with me."
- "Better other-centered acceptance of their disagreements than self-centered denouncement of them."
- "My values are neither superior nor sacred compared to others, and their opinions warrant a review as much as mine."
- "The wider the disagreement and the more unconventional others views are compared to mine, the more I can learn - if I play my cards right by encountering and actually encouraging others' alternative expressions."
- "Defending others' right to their own opinion is in my best interest because it encourages more open, balanced relationships where we both have input."
- "Standing up for others' right to disagree argues against personal insecurity and can help to build self-confidence."
- "Knowing that I don't have to rate or define myself by others' disagreements with me frees me up to encourage mutual discussions in the service of greater relationship lubrication."
- "Not hassling others when they take issue with me makes for a better give-and-take relationship in the future."
- "Welcoming another's opinion though it may clash with mine leaves the welcome door open for freer and clearer expressions in the future."
- "If I truly want to get to know someone in a holistic way, I would do well to encourage their opinions, however divergent from mine they are."

Playing by the rules while defending others' right to agree and disagree with you generates harmony, respect, better mutual understanding, and more learning. Giving consent and tolerance to others exercising their right to disagree avoids a forked-tongue approach that implies, "Save time - see it my way." Sometimes the best offense is a good defense. To unangrily defend others' right to take exception to your views avoids the offensive feelings that are often created when inevitable disagreements lead to the death of free-will to the onset of "my will" (be done). (Un)angrily defending another's right to disagree is the offense that can prevent angry offensiveness.

Note. From *You Can Control Your Anger! 21 Ways To Do It* by Bill Borcherdt. Copyright © 2000, Professional Resource Exchange, Inc., P.O. Box 15560, Sarasota, FL 34277-1560.

Chapter 14 Review Questions

1. How does a decent respect for individual differences pre-
    vent anger?

2. What does agreeing to disagree mean for you and how
    can it prevent anger?

3. How does high frustration tolerance (HFT) contrast with
    low frustration tolerance (LFT)?

4. What do ideas of parity refer to?

5. Why is interdependence an important concept in mini-
    mizing anger?

CHAPTER 15

First Come, First Serve: Hurt as It Precedes and Is Attended To Before Anger

Tracking anger as an emotional disturbance often does not follow a straight line. Its understanding and correction is often found off the beaten track in the form of the hurt that precedes it. This chapter will emphasize the value in servicing what comes first, the angry chicken or the hurtful egg. It will discuss the egg (hurt) before the chicken (anger) theory; in other words, viewing hurt as the prelude, the foreplay to anger. Anger is often disguised hurt and is presented as such because:

1. *Anger energizes, hurt saps energy.* When the choice is reviewed, feeling listless and lethargic by making oneself feel hurt, and feeling full of steam and vigor by inducing anger, the more animated feelings of anger usually win out.
2. *Anger is more visible.* Most conclude that they can better get their message across with an active display of anger than with a passive onset of hurt. They believe that anger will help others to take note of all the important things they have to say.

3. *Anger provides a surge of power and control, while hurt offers doses of impotence and weakness.* A blast of energy is created with anger while feelings of inertia accompany hurt.

4. *Anger is more identifiable.* You can hang your hat on anger and its skyrocketing effects. Hurt is a ghostlike, mystery emotion that seems to come from parts unknown as it quickly takes the wind out of your emotional sails. Hurt leaves you breathless, while anger has you breathing hard while building up its onslaught. Hurt seems not to be an emotional resource; anger appears as if it is.

5. *Anger makes is easier to blame others; hurt contains portions of self-blame.* Many prefer to angrily blame others than to hurtfully blame themselves.

6. *Hurt makes it appear that one is vulnerable to emotional hardship.* Anger gives off a Rock of Gibraltar scent. Using anger as a mechanism of grandiose expression, the appearance of invulnerability is made to be the charted course.

7. *Anger is more socially acceptable than hurt.* We live in a society where aggression is deified and passiveness is devilified. Those who express their aggression within society's norms are put up on a pedestal, while those who hold back are ignored, at best. The values of our social group reflect a permissiveness toward many forms of anger expression which is gullibly absorbed by the angry- rather than the hurt-acting person.

8. *Anger disguises personal insecurity.* Lacking self-confidence, anger serves as a smokescreen that makes it appear that you are sure of yourself, when you are really shaking in your boots.

9. *Anger provides an exalted, holier-than-thou thrashing of another, often as a secretive way to camouflage unworthier-than-all feelings.* Ego heavens are made to arise so as to prevent ego hells from taking over. Angry-acting people often prefer the self-righteous pedestal they place themselves on to the snake belly depths they, lacking anger,

otherwise would feel. Anger is often an ego trip that is too tempting to ground oneself on.

10. *Anger is more easily released than hurt.* Anger is more an act of impulse, which makes its expression ripe for itchy fingers. With hurt, time is taken to think if not brood about your misfortune; anger is a more ever-ready feeling.

11. *Anger is more likely to reveal low frustration tolerance (LFT) tendencies than hurt;* that is, "I can't stand it when others treat me badly," and "I can't stand it that I am not coping better with this terrible matter." This inclination to exaggerate the difficulty of seeing your way through a troublesome situation is more likely to fuel anger than hurt.

12. *Anger creates the illusion of strength.* Angry-acting people are of feeble thought in their view of self. Presto! And with the accompaniment of anger they feel strong, if not all-powerful. This godlike disillusionment takes precedence over down-in-the-dumps hurt.

13. *Anger is easier to admit than the self-pity that is often at the base of hurt.* Self-pity is a woeful emotion that is perhaps the most difficult of the feeling states to own up to. Anger is often seen as a more "adult" emotion than the "let the baby have its milk," childlike self-pity feeling.

14. *Angry arrogance as supposed anointment is hard to resist.* Angry people have traits of arrogance whose expression anger conveniences. My views are all right and yours are all wet form the foundation of this black-or-white mentality. At their peak, angry-ridden people believe themselves to be anointed in the sense of their rules being golden, which puts them, by their own distorted thinking, at the center of the universe - or so the fairy tale goes.

In summary, power, control, strength, and invulnerability are sought after in the angry hunt while fear, self-depreciation, and insecurity are to be avoided in this search. All this ego, esteem-seeking efforts of futility can be avoided by first attending to the frequent backbone of anger, hurt. Better tracing of anger to its origins in hurt can be done by:

(a) Entering your emotional analysis with a philosophy of admittance. Call a spade a spade and hurt, hurt - not anger. Acknowledging hurt may seem like a difficult thing to do, but in doing so you can begin to more thoroughly abolish anger by undercutting the hurt that preceded it. By these computations anger is disallowed from getting out of its starting block.

(b) Identify the precise self-made conclusions that create hurt. These could include:

- "What is wrong with me that I can't get others to treat me kinder?"
- "What is wrong with me for not being able to cope more soundly with others' unpleasant sounds?"
- "Poor me for missing out on what was an important goal."
- "I was promised cooperation; how horrible I feel that such promise was betrayed."
- "Woe is me for once again losing out."
- "What a loser I am for losing."
- "What a horror it is that life refuses to give me all the things that I miss."
- "It seems things should be easier for me than they are."
- "I try my best to get along, and it's awful when others don't follow suit."
- "I give and I give, and then I give some more with a minute return at best on my efforts - then they wonder why I whine so much."

(c) Identify alternate conclusions that cut through hurt so that you don't feel cut upon. Examples are:

- "Life doesn't have to give me all the things that I miss."
- "If I lose I don't have to view myself as a loser nor feel sorry for myself."
- "So I'm not the one person in the universe who gets everything his or her little heart desires."
- "If I try, sometimes I will succeed, sometimes I will fail; if I don't try I will never succeed - but in either case I can fully accept myself."
- "Better that I expect less from others."
- "Woe is me-ism causes me to stew and not do - a real breeding ground for making myself feel hurt."
- "I don't have to take matters of failure or disapproval personally."
- "I don't have to define, rate, or judge myself by others' conduct and opinions. Such evaluations illustrate what they value - they don't represent or illustrate me."
- "Being left out is no fun, but I can live with exclusion."
- "Matters of life and love are not required to be any easier than they are."

(d) Develop an action component to your remedial efforts. First, identify the philosophical roots of hurt as they thrive in self-blame and self-pity and, at the behavioral level, inaction and do-nothingism. Do, don't brood; stay active on your own behalf. Those who take on and practice a philosophy of enlightened self-interest find little time to hurtfully agonize about their disappointments and inconveniences. Examples of getting a move on it rather than sitting on your problems are:

- Seek out how and where you can reclaim what it is you lost; for example, a love relationship, a job, an award.
- Seek out an activity you wish to master but have never tried before, such as playing a guitar, or learning about computers.
- Greet others rather than wait for them to greet you.
- Take a class that could give you another life's advantage, such as increasing your chances for promotion or teaching you how to be more assertive.
- Volunteer to help someone.
- Visit someone whom you haven't seen in some time.
- Visit a place you have never been to or haven't been to in some time.
- Write out a list of all the things you would like to experience in the approximate time you have left on this earth and start to engage yourself in doing some of them.
- Exercise regularly.
- Read a book on a topic you have been wanting to learn more about.
- Call a friend or relative in a distant city.
- Contribute your time to a cause you find worthy.
- Try to get to know someone better that you deem interesting.
- Eat a food you have seldom or never tried before.
- Brainstorm other things under the heading of doing things differently and doing different things - and keep adding to this list of pleasures and challenges.

People think, feel, and act (TFA) their way into their hurtful feelings, and it would be important to develop ideas that TFA their way out of their feeling slumber. This chapter has presented ideas that emphasize attending to anger by dissolving the hurt that often precedes anger's appearance. By proceeding with anger and its origins in hurt, you can experience the proceeds from untying this disturbance duo. This "first things first, tending to hurt first" approach puts your emotional well-being first, keeping your hurt and anger at arm's length.

Note. From *You Can Control Your Anger! 21 Ways To Do It* by Bill Borcherdt. Copyright © 2000, Professional Resource Exchange, Inc., P.O. Box 15560, Sarasota, FL 34277-1560.

Chapter 15 Review Questions

1. What comes first, the chicken or the egg; the hurt or the anger?

2. Why is anger often disguised hurt?

3. What are some self-stated solutions that cause hurt?

4. What is the action component to remedying hurt?

5. How is anger a holier-than-thou-based emotion?

CHAPTER 16

What Moses Accidentally on Purpose Left on the Mount: The 11th Commandment and Its Bias and Basis in Anger Control

Dissecting anger is important in that it can reveal the anatomy of what you're up against in trying to regulate it or, in Rational Emotive Behavior Therapy terms, to dissolve it. What is even more important is to identify and put into practice the philosophical values handiwork that has the capability to demolishing this most dangerous of all emotions. It may be that the future of the human race will be contingent upon the ability of this species to provide a remedy for this self-administered condition. To do anger in before it does us in may be like a race to the finish line that is almost too close to call. The 11th commandment is about the capacity to begin to understand how anger is self-created and what can be done so that the human race can do what can be done to interrupt and curtail it. The 11th commandment reads as follows:

- "My will be done."
- "Everybody is entitled to my opinion!"
- "My values are sacred and superior."

- "Thou shalt have no values besides mine."
- "You, buster, have no right to go against my heavenly ideas."
- "You don't have free-will - you have *my* will!"

If Moses had had more of a brain in his head, he would have taken this angry verdict with him, tried to measure its negative impact, and made a good effort to discourage its "Be (un)fruitful and multiply" effects. From there the human race - minus anger - could have lived happily ever after. But as reality would have it, the dictates of the 11th commandment all too frequently reign as the supreme guideline for gauging interactions between humans. Unless it is better regulated the future of the species is up for grabs.

This is so because, all too often, anger leads to rage, fury, and aggression. Incorporated under the umbrella of anger, as expressed through the ultimatum that Moses neglected to bring on home, are the following components of this most harmful of all emotions. Let's say we agree to forgive Moses for his oversight in a similar manner that we could forgive self and others when the wrong road is taken. That way we could evaporate this listing of anger's mechanics in a way that allows life to go on more peacefully. Angers' makeup that blocks making up includes this array of lethal dimensions:

1. *Demandingness is at the top of its class in anger production and at the bottom of its class in addressing social harmony.* "Be reasonable, do it my way" increases hostile friction between self and social group.
2. *"Two-year-oldism" is exercised as an option when individuals stomp their feet, rant and rave, moan and groan, or hoot and howl when not getting their own way.* Such childlike behavior creates a dramatic scene, usually without noticeable productive results.
3. *Grandiosity or "center of the universism" disclaims others' opportunity to include their two cents' worth because it*

proclaims that everything the self-glorified individual wants, he or she MUST have, and any ideas to the contrary don't count. Anger is created by such alleged self-anointed provisions and can be dissolved by taking yourself and your proclamations off your self-righteous pedestal.

4. *Condemnation.* Perhaps as much as anything, anger is a damnation of another human being. Such subhuman artillery is often used as justification for anger expression.

5. *Punitiveness.* Because you betray my values as you must not, not only are you to be condemned as the villain that you most certainly are, but also, for not so good measure, you are to be punished so that you think twice before committing an infraction against my sacred rules and regulations again.

6. *Necessitizing means that you deem it absolutely necessary that the world and those in it fully go to bat on behalf of your almighty beliefs and that you will strike them (out) if they stay in the dugout as a means of not patronizing your views.* Believing that others are mandated by need and necessity to accommodate your values creates anger.

7. *Essentialism.* Here again requirements take on life-threatening proportions. Arbitrary definitions for happiness and survival are presumed to exist; without their essential presence, life cannot be made to go on. Anger is often kicked into gear in an effort to control for these presumed essentials.

8. *Porcupinism.* Try to make love with a porcupine sometime and find out what a fatal attraction you have on your hands - and legs, arms, face, and so on. It just plain isn't much fun to associate with someone who comes to the relationship armed with iced pricklies. This feature of anger expression will leave you painted into a corner away from your social group.

9. *Sweet revenge turned sour.* Angry-acting people often go for the jugular vein when countering someone who has the gall to think and act differently from them. In the proc-

ess of their counterantagonisms they momentarily feel good while lapping up the initial sweet taste of revenge. However, they continue on with their bottomless-pit, get-even riff-raff. By the time they finally realize that too much is not enough in terms of (seeming) sweet revenge, they have gotten themselves emotionally out of hand and have only succeeded in taking a bad situation and making it worse.

10. *Intolerance.* Convincing yourself that not only do you not like and approve of certain things and people that are and go against your way of navigating life, but also that you absolutely can't stand such rebuttal, breeds intolerance, which in turn breeds contempt, hostility, and, alas - aggression.

11. *Tit-for-tat, score-keeping, don't-get-mad-get-even philosophies.* Angry-acting people tend to fight fire with fire, opting for the notion of an eye for an eye and a tooth for a tooth. They soon forget that a get-even mentality often results in a lot of blind toothless people walking around.

12. *"Hardening of the oughteries" ideas that focus on how others "oughta" treat you often go against the reality that others will more often than not select and discriminate against you.* When such "ought to"s contrast with reality, emotional sparks are likely to fly to the detriment of your long-range happiness and survival.

13. *Shouldhood.* Others should be the way they are, not according to how you think they "should" be. Avoiding shouldhood lends itself to undamning acceptance of others as they are, not as you think they should be. A more permissive stance will likely put anger on the run so that its negative effects are distanced from your emotional well-being.

14. *Musthood is linked to shouldhood in kind and also in degree: It carries more emphatic and potentially stronger emotional and behavioral consequences.* The strength of

one's "musts" are in proportion to the strength of one's anger. It is easier to retract to your preferences and desires with a should statement than it is with a must, which implies more dogma with its underlying current of "dig in your heels."

15. *Emotional dependency.* At the core of most anger is this emotional flypaper that is prompted by a philosophy of desperation. It is nearly impossible to gain and maintain an angry state toward another unless you first make yourself dependent on him or her for one or more of the following:

- Love
- Encouragement
- Approval
- Affirmation
- Acceptance
- Cooperation
- Emotional support
- Understanding
- Communication
- Agreement
- Reciprocation

If you didn't think that you needed or required any of these 11 seeming human "needs" there would be no foundation for the 11th commandment from which to build your case for anger, hostility, resentment, vindictiveness, and punitiveness.

16. *Arrogance and self-righteousness.* These two common character traits of the human condition are an integral part of an anger build-up. Reeking with the idea that "I'm all right and you're all wrong," the arrogant-acting know-it-all will wreck many a relationship possibility.

17. *Bigotry.* Last but certainly not least in charting the anatomy of anger is the black-or-white, all-or-nothing, this-way-or-that-type thinking that starts the angry road more traveled. When combined with fanaticism, bigotry is a powerful, destructive force that takes no prisoners en route to destroying those who get in the way, or who even have the gumption to skeptically question the sacred cows.

In that anger is philosophically, value, and not circumstantially based or interpersonally woven it can be dissolved and therefore near depleted from the human equation by correcting irrational ideas. What follows is a review of the irrational ideas that support the 17 dimensions of anger just reviewed and their rational counters that can contribute to abolishing angry contraband.

DIMENSIONS OF ANGER	IRRATIONAL IDEAS	RATIONAL COUNTERS
1. *Demandingness*	"I have to have my own way and you have to give it to me (or else I'll clobber you and despise you until the day that I die - and I hope that it's soon.")"	"I naturally would like my own way but it is your prerogative as to whether you want to give it to me."
2. *Two-year-oldism*	"The world revolves around me and I'll whine and scream, shake and bake until it finally acknowledges this fact."	"I am not a big freaking baby nor do I have to push my emotions to the limit when the world doesn't devote itself to making me happy."
3. *Grandiosity*	"My will and words are the Alpha and Omega, the beginning and the end."	"My will and words are important to me but are not perched above all others."
4. *Condemnation*	"Others are to be berated and looked down upon when they trespass on my values."	"There is not a 'no trespassing' sign on my values and it would be wise of me not to foolishly attempt to plant one there."
5. *Punitiveness*	"Others should be punished for extending themselves beyond the bounds of what I know is the right thing to do - vengeance is mine, saith I."	"It's difficult to punish another in the short run without punishing yourself in the long run."

DIMENSIONS OF ANGER *(Cont'd)*	IRRATIONAL IDEAS *(Cont'd)*	RATIONAL COUNTERS *(Cont'd)*
6. *Necessitizing*	"It's necessary that the world bend my way, and when it doesn't it's necessary to (a) get myself bent out of shape and (b) depreciate myself for my overreactions."	"It's nice but it's a distant second to believe that it is necessary to have items on my wish list fall into my lap."
7. *Essentialism*	"Happiness cannot be gained, and I must be and remain miserable when what I deem to be essential is nowhere to be found."	"I may not be as happy if I am unable to do exactly with my life what I want to, but that is a far cry from totally abandoning the good I can gain from my time on earth."
8. *Porcupinism*	"I'll show those who go against my wishes by using my negative demeanor and sharp tongue to keep them at a distance."	"Sharp flattery will get me further than sharp manners or tongue any day; the first shows maturity, the second is but child's play."
9. *Sweet revenge turned sour*	"I'll get even and I could care less if I cut off my nose to spite my face along the way."	"Revenge is bitter, not sweet, and there are enough potholes in life already without me inventing more."
10. *Intolerance*	"I can't stand it when others replace my values with their own. Who do they think they are, God or somebody?"	"Disappointments are not disasters when others frown upon or otherwise throw cold water on my values."
11. *Tit-for-tat, get-even methods of influence*	"Monkey see, monkey do is fine with me; two can play that game."	"I can proceed to a neutral corner rather than stand at center stage fighting out differences of opinion."

DIMENSIONS OF ANGER *(Cont'd)*	IRRATIONAL IDEAS *(Cont'd)*	RATIONAL COUNTERS *(Cont'd)*
12. *Hardening of the oughteries*	"Others oughta treat me with no lapses in kindness and consideration, and they oughta be darned when they don't."	"Others oughta be the way that they are because they are that way - whether I like it or not is beside the point."
13. *Shouldhood*	"Others should act in accordance to what I believe is best."	"Others can provide all the emotional interference that they want - regardless of what my little heart desires."
14. *Musthood*	"Others must act as I declare them to."	"Others can act against my personal beliefs about my King James version of life. Whether I decide to like it, lump it, or anger myself about it is up to me."
15. *Emotional dependency*	"I absolutely *need* certain things from others, and when they don't provide it, they are responsible for my unhappiness."	"Others shining up to me by monitoring and providing for my desires is a terrific thing when done, but it is seldom the case due to others focusing on their own more than intermittent problems and disturbances."
16. *Arrogance and self-righteousness*	"My values are head and shoulders above others, and these same others should be more eager to know what they are."	"My values are significant to me but I can understand that they often may not hold water for others - after all, aren't all people different?"

DIMENSIONS OF ANGER *(Cont'd)*	IRRATIONAL IDEAS *(Cont'd)*	RATIONAL COUNTERS *(Cont'd)*
17. *Bigotry*	"What the world can use is more people who know absolutely beyond a shadow of a doubt that they know what they are doing and can get their centerpieces of life across to others - even if it means shoving them down others' throats."	"What the world may profit from is more people who have decent respect for individual difference, realizing and practicing the notion that one size doesn't fit all."

There you have it, 17 dead ringers for anger. These look-alikes will leave you emotionally reeling unless leveled in the confinement of your mind. What angry-acting people don't realize is that they don't run the universe yet - though they may be feverishly and foolishly trying and vying to do so. It may seem difficult to make up with another or make peace with yourself, but as hard as it may be to dissolve anger, it's harder not to. As a species we may be in our 11th hour in getting a bead on relinquishing anger. Until anger is made to evaporate, risks of war, genocide, nationalism, and domestic violence remain ongoing risk factors. Moses, it's all your fault! Had you not forgotten to include the 11th commandment - "my will be done" - we could more easily acknowledge the faults in all of us while surrendering the blame within and between humans. Moses' error of omission deserves reprimand without damnation. With this more tolerant, permissive way we can clear a better trail for ourselves in doing our own work by accidentally on purpose remembering to not forget to take on a nonblaming, undamning acceptance view of self in relationship to others.

Note. From *You Can Control Your Anger! 21 Ways To Do It* by Bill Borcherdt. Copyright © 2000, Professional Resource Exchange, Inc., P.O. Box 15560, Sarasota, FL 34277-1560.

Chapter 16 Review Questions

1. What is the 11th commandment?

2. How is condemnation part of the 11th commandment?

3. What does necessitizing mean for you?

4. What are three dimensions of emotional dependency?

5. Is anger circumstantially or philosophically based, and why?

CHAPTER 17

The Wounded Animal Mentality:
Ways To Avoid the Hunt and Hurt

The choice between living with a caged animal or one with the freedom to roam would be an easy decision to make. Yet when this choice is figuratively applied to human relationships, the choice often is not made to be easy as it appears to be when applied to animals. The three main premises of this chapter are described below:

1. *When in close, regular association with someone it would be in your best interest to supply the provisions - that is, cooperation rather than conflict, kindness rather than criticism, pleasantness rather than harshness, and friendliness rather than fickleness - that would likely please enormously the people you share space with.* That way, you make it convenient for others to put themselves in a more favorable mood - making your day happier in that others would be more fun to be around. By giving off prickly messages, you encourage others to take your negative comments and sultry actions personally, making themselves feel hurtfully wounded in an emotional sense. Contributing to and living with such an emotionally wounded person is a monster that you can do without and can, by playing your patronizing

cards right, afford to do without having a not-so-helpful hand in creating.

2. *The door can swing both ways if you let it.* Just as your words, when taken too seriously by others, can result in their feeling hurt, so too can others' words and deeds made all important lead to you making yourself feel hurtfully wounded. Regardless of whether it be you or the other who feels the hurt, such feelings of weakness are a step away from the fantasy feeling of strength that anger is falsely concluded to offer. The wounded person, whether you or the other, is often quick to translate the empty, lifeless, impotent feeling of hurt into anger. This is accomplished by hanging your hat on blaming the other and holding the other accountable for the hurt to begin with; for example, "You're making me feel bad by not giving me the kind treatment that I need from you, so therefore you, as rotten a person as you are, are responsible for my problems and disturbances." This blaming notion has a self-pitying ring to it as it triggers anger toward the person deemed as lax in providing the resources that you have defined as necessary. Such anger feelings and expressions then perfume feelings of insecurity, vulnerability, and hurt temporarily. They supply the nerve gas to more forcefully represent yourself, but in truth make self-doubts and other unsureties that leave you gasping for emotional air - breaths that anger, as a more energizing emotion, provides.

3. *What can be done to relinquish such fencing in and taking pot shots at the wounded animal.* Such restraint can prove helpful whether you are at the sending end of contributing to a wounded companion with all the disadvantages of living thereof, or at the receiving end of someone shooting at you to emotionally kill you and you wish to avoid giving him or her a pound of your flesh.

Because humans are gregarious by nature, they form associations and attachments to one another. If in the context of your getting to know another, you get wind of his or her Achilles' heel and sore spots, it would be better to not encourage a fuller opening up of the wound. For instance, if you discover that your associate is psychologically allergic to certain nicknames or adverse to reminders of past mistakes, it would be far better to avoid such labeling and/or reminding. "Rubbing it in" tendencies may result in the other wanting to "rub you out." Rather than pouring fuel onto the fire so that you may feast on the other's sensitivities, it would be advisable to skip over such a roast, or in the end it may be you who is eaten alive. It is not wise to rekindle as open for discussion negative reminders that help in activating others' overreactive tendencies. Once the wounded animal is agitated by you hitting below its belt, life is often turned into a mudslinging match, with your hurtable associate going to far ends to seek and deliver your vulnerabilities. If he or she is successful, you end up with two raging bulls who, though feasting on each other, become skeletons from their own preying. Each destroys himself or herself emotionally in efforts to destroy the other, being left with the common bond of mutual misery.

It takes two to fight and an issue to fight about. Winston Churchill said, "Nothing in life is so exhilarating as to be shot at without result." Protect yourself from making yourself into the wounded animal by not personalizing vicious attempts to sway and slay you. Anyone who would try to inflict wounds on an innocent bystander is likely to be miserable to begin with. To deny, get yourself defensive, or counterattack snide hostility will only accumulate more dirty laundry than was originally piled up. Take a step back rather than two steps forward by doing yourself a favor: remind yourself, "How unfortunate that my associate is acting like such a wounded animal; now, the task for me is to create a distance between him and me without unduly upsetting myself about his problems and disturbance - yet attempting to have a fair amount of compassion for my wounded, hurting associate." Why compassion? Because it beats other feeling states, such as other pity, angry self-pity, hostility, and so on toward the bad-acting, yet hurting one all to hell - if your purpose is to live happier. Lacking compassion for the disturbed person is akin to becoming the disturbed person by way of philosophy and emotion; that is, if you damn someone who damns you or treat someone rude for treating you rudely, you merely duplicate his or her errors. "Monkey see, monkey do" lacks creativity and self-reliance, and an independent other's sore spots can be replaced with purposefully overlooking in decision-making capacities. Specific suggestions for preventing yourself from hunting and attempting to inflict pain upon those you associate with include:

1. *Consider the backlash factor.* Knowing that the wounded animal will try to track you down and possibly spend the rest of his or her life retaliating against your shoddy behavior is reason enough not to make war with him or her.

2. *Realize that such misconduct merely strengthens your own feelings of hostility.* Practicing vindictive behavior strengthens the influence of your own hostility and anger in approaching life. Infiltration of hostility often leading to aggression will likely turn against your best interests. As you get better at expressing such brutality, your connections with others get worse.

3. *Take stock of the ramifications of your porcupine behavior in your contacts with your social group.* Associates are likely to boycott and disadvantage you by pulling back resources due to their resentment of the open season leveled against them.

4. *Patronize, don't pot shoot.* Far better that you fudge certain differences with your cohorts when not doing so prompts arguments where either you both lose, or you lose by winning, that is, you "prove" a point, and win the battle but lose the war against disharmony. Find shades of gray when it warms the cockles of another's heart rather than

shooting for and beating to death the heart of your differences. Finding and acknowledging at least some truth to your acquaintance's statements that are miles apart from your beliefs on the matter can prevent the chilling and killing of an otherwise reasonable relationship.

5. *Refuse to hit below the belt.* A huge majority of people make themselves overly sensitive about one thing or another, for example, their big nose, their little/big breasts, education deficiencies, flawed family background, and so on. Avoid conversing or teasing about those sensitive areas because such ammunition used will only lead to opening up old wounds - enticing the wounded animal even more.

6. *Embrace strengths, not weaknesses and insecurities.* Zero in on what your associate can do rather than highlight his or her deficiencies. Challenge yourself to avoid that which others make themselves self-conscious about while staying more focused on others' traits and achievements that they take pride in.

7. *Itemize what you have to lose.* See that whatever short-run dominance you might feel by emotionally "picking on" someone is but a temporary drop in the bucket when considering embittered longer range consequences from your ally turned enemy.

8. *See what you have to gain.* Harsh words and deeds turneth away kindness, and kind words and deeds turneth away wrath. The percentages are or are not in your favor, depending on your choice - and the choice is yours. Just as more bees are likely to be gained with honey than with vinegar, so too is more kindness likely to come back to you with investments of pleasantry rather than wrath.

9. *Appreciate the time cap of life.* Life is a limited feature showing only once, with no dress rehearsals prior to the big top. Why not spend your limited time in a way that better assures exchanges of kindness protection with your social group. Rather than do things against them that en-

courage alienation, do things for them that better lubricate contacts with them. Just as it is more fun to be around a tamed, friendly animal than a wounded one, so too is the quality of the one life you will ever have upgraded by friendly, supportive persuasion toward your peers.

10. *Strengthen the value of (preferably unangry) restraint and be aware of how it is more likely to set the table for solutions rather than multiply problems.* Restraint won't kill you, though angry expression might. Chances are, if you don't favorably influence another with patience and restraint, it is near impossible that you will with antagonism and ass chewing. Set a precedent by making up your mind to use your hostile inclinations to work on your own mental health. Counter tendencies toward anger, rage, fury, and passive and active aggressive misconduct by building a case for grace, tolerance, acceptance, and forgiveness so as to pave the way for staying out of harm's way.

11. *Sidestep a self-esteem, self-worth model.* Ordinarily, when in the throes of anger, individuals feel like God almighty, better than the scum who differ with them. Self-esteem skyrockets as angry-acting people believe that they are to be deified and their detractors devilified. Self-proving has its paws in a huge majority of human relationship problems and, when avoided, minimizes desires to hunt and hurt others. Angry-acting people tend to truly believe that they run the universe, are 100% correct, and therefore see themselves as angels and their loyal opposition as devils. By avoiding rating people you can often avoid anger and aggression.

12. *Distinguish between a slip and a major setback.* Acting asininely toward your social group doesn't make you an ass. If you try harder to take a gentler person stance with others and sometimes falter, don't put yourself down for your error but instead push yourself back onto the wagon

that you pushed yourself off of, vowing to do better in the future (rather than condemning yourself in the present).

13. *Concentrate more on making fewer errors in the future.* Instead of raking yourself over the coals for your prickly conduct, focus on learning from and correcting those mistakes in the future. Correction, yes! Condemnation, no!

Specific suggestions to prevent yourself from becoming the wounded animal in the face of others' embitteredness, animosity, and taunting follow:

1. *Avoid the addictive tendency to retaliate.* Anger expression can feel oh, so good at the time it is splattered out, but it is likely to result in oh, so bad-type consequences. The problem is that something that feels so good in the present has a longing, a nostalgia to go back to it even if it's not good for you. There is a feel-good, immediate-rush, empowerment experience associated with anger that can make it build-up and make its expression difficult to resist.

2. *Don't take it personally.* Taunters will treat others similar to the way they treat you. Others' conduct toward you says a lot about their personality makeup, for better or for worse, and says nothing about you as a person. In fact, others will tease and target you for the same reason some will feel pleased being with and accepting you.

3. *Practice empathy training.* Have a sense for the weak, defensive, insecure nature of the aggressive offender and try to develop a sense of compassion toward the wounded animal. Say to yourself, "Isn't it unfortunate that my peer is acting so badly. How miserable and down on himself he must be, otherwise he would have better things to do than to try to disrupt my peace and quiet; now how can I protect myself from his nonsensical-acting ways without getting myself hung up in and on his obvious problems and disturbances?"

4. *Don't become the enemy.* Find better ways to curtail and dissolve your potential feelings of anger than retaliation.

5. *Respect your nemesis's fear.* Angry people are fearful people, afraid that they aren't going to prove themselves - specifically their absolute superiority over all who cross their path. They try to vanish with anger their felt inferiority. They are hurting psychologically and desperately want to pass the buck of their misgivings about themselves; they blame and look down on others, wrongly believing that if they would cease such defensive tactics they would be required to blame and look down on themselves.

6. *Don't exaggerate.* Words are words, they are not sticks and stones and therefore cannot break your bones unless you sharpen them up and throw gasoline on the (in)significance of them. Others gossiping about you or more directly criticizing you does not require you to throw gasoline on such uneventful events made eventful. See that being selected against and being criticized, though not the grandest of all human experiences, is certainly tolerable and bearable and exposure to less than desirable antics of others is highly unlikely to require that you be given a decent burial.

7. *Physically remove yourself from the hunting grounds.* Literally turning your back and exiting others' attempts to trap or figuratively shoot at you can be handled by a simple shrug of the shoulders en route to abandoning the hunting land. Few like to be ignored, and, by leaving, you leave other people shadow-boxing with themselves. If you talk to the telephone post and it doesn't talk back, it's highly likely that you will stop talking to and trying to provoke it.

8. *Head anger off at the pass by admitting to the hurt that often precedes it.* Acknowledging feeling feeble in the face of others' attempts to make you not so fair game for their barbs and bellerings more accurately owns up to the facts of your feelings. Forget about and forgive yourself for not feeling strong each and every time that you are ver-

bally abused. It is not necessary to feel strength all or anytime when in the heat of battle. Take pressure off yourself by seeing that though it would be nice to be able to unhurtfully stand up and be counted when accosted with another's thistletold comments, it isn't necessary. By leading with hurt that is accurate, you can sidestep anger that is inaccurate. "You hurt me - you bastard" can be replaced with, "I'm making myself feel hurt and weak, now what can I do to change the route of my self-administered impotence or not hassle myself or in any way put myself down for presently not being capable of bargaining from other than this weakened position?"

Those with the wounded animal mentality, both the hunter and the hunted, have emotional problems. Whether it be you or others who are on the prowl, get out of the hunt and avoid the hurt and anger that is often made to go along with the open season territory. Avoidance of such interfering emotions allows you to keep your emotional wits about you by winding down rather than winding up this wounded, a wound for a wound, wounded animal mentality.

Chapter 17 Review Questions

1.　Why is it to your advantage to treat others with respect?

2.　What is the backlash factor?

3.　Why can patronization be a good thing?

4.　What does "refusing to hit below the belt" mean?

5.　How will not taking things personally contribute to you not making yourself into a wounded animal?

CHAPTER 18

Begrudgedness: Sixteen Ways To Unglue Rather Than Extend The Chip On Your Shoulder

Walking around as if you have a chip glued to your shoulder or a ramrod shoved up your keister is not a very rewarding way to go through life. Unmannerly ways of signaling to your social group your grudges against them and or against life and the universe itself will likely boomerang. It is difficult to act in shoddy, grudge-filled ways without hurting yourself. If you act like a porcupine toward your associates, they are likely to get the hostile message and turn against you. By sawing off the chip on your shoulder and by trimming off sharpened quills, you can be more assured of better days ahead with those that you share living space with.

Holding onto a grudge for dear life can kill an otherwise potentially pleasant climate. The mechanics, the anatomy of begrudged displays of antagonisms include:

1. *Self-pity.* Woe is me Mister and Ms-ism implies that you believe that the world and people in it are picking on you, and your pity bucket response represents a demand that they not do so. Because others are for themselves, the universe

is impartial, and it would be in your best interest to be for yourself rather than pity yourself.

2. *Pouting.* Going without is one thing, in fact is often a given part of the human condition. Pouting about going without is taking a circumstance where the world and people in it are frustrating you and making it worse by moaning and groaning about the deprivation.

3. *Sulking is akin to pouting but perhaps paints a clearer picture of angry disenchantment.* More childlike drama is seen in sulking as an active ingredient of holding a grudge.

4. *Sullenness can be an especially fixed emotional and behavioral state that portrays grumpiness and begrudgedness.* To hang on for dear life a sullen temperament can contribute to the death of a relationship.

5. *Self-indulgence runs through all of the above as such expressions provide a peculiar, unusual sense of smug satisfaction.* It is almost as if the begrudgful antics serve notice to the rest of the world that it is being punished by the indulger's self-centered expressions. When my son Bill was age 5, I corrected him in a way that he disapproved of. He proceeded to voice his upset by threatening, "Now to get you mad, I'm going to sit here and be bored!" Such self-centered and center-of-attention behavior runs through the philosophy of the grudgeful one.

6. *Grandiosity.* Grudge holders are really angry that the world refuses to cater to them. When not given everything they want and when not protected from everything that they don't want, they tend to wear their demand to be treated partially on their sleeve and shoulder.

7. *Self-righteousness.* Upon declaring that they are right and the rest of the world is wrong, those that hold a grudge stick their nose in the air as an arrogant display of know-it-all-ism. They then harbor a grudge because they can't understand why others don't want to adopt the absolute truth as seen through their eyes.

8. *Animosity.* Holding against others their reluctance to buy into your school of thought can create grudge matches too numerous to mention.
9. *Sense of entitlement.* The belief that everybody is entitled to my opinion because my values are sacred holds those who do not opt for this insistence in ongoing disrepute.
10. *Clammerings for fairness and deservingness.* Demanding that you get what you want and think you deserve as opposed to what you get sets the stage for opposing forces begrudging one another.

Sawing off the chip on your shoulder before it does you in can be accomplished with these antibegrudging ideas and suggestions:

1. *Take the pout out of going without.* View being deprived of what you want as an unharrow rather than an absolute harrow. Whether it be another's approval, material gains, a desired accomplishment, or some other advantage in life, accept that a large part of the human condition is going without and that holding a grudge about it makes the load even heavier.
2. *Accept that what goes around frequently doesn't come around.* Squelch the notion that others will always get their due. See that the universe is impartial and objective - just plain uncaring as to whether justice and mercy triumph. That way you will be less grudge-filled when you put your best foot forward and get it stepped on.
3. *Minimize magical thinking.* Those who hold grudges often missile themselves into believing that somehow their ill will is hurting those their resentment is directed toward. Little is further from the truth in that your ill-willed thoughts have no way of wiggling inside someone else's gut and causing them emotional harm. Such primitive, Neanderthal thinking implies that by energizing yourself with em-

bittered thinking you can use such gusto to influence if not change undesirable circumstances and those behind same. However, any changes made out of anger and aftermath grudge holding are likely to be for the worse; it is difficult to hold a grudge against the world and people in it without hurting yourself.

4. *Sprightly and steadfastly put frustration behind you.* The best time to change a bad habit is as soon as possible after you notice that it is or could soon become a problem for you. As soon as you sense you are starting to wallow in holding a grudge with all its dimensions described earlier, stop! Resolve that this hostile bandit is not going to be allowed to steal your happiness.

5. *Use heavy doses of consequential thinking.* Plainly ask yourself, "Where does this contrary style of relating get me?" See that when you let others get to you and you quietly but begrudgingly try to get back at them, you are taking a bad situation and making it worse!

6. *Find and focus upon the good in the bad.* Rather than brood about unfairness and injustice from another, holistically give credit to the mannerly aspects of your relationship with the other. Don't lose sight of his or her favorable side or you will lose out on the advantages of experiencing what those items are.

7. *Forcefully, if necessary, produce countering pleasant behaviors.* Being kind helps to neutralize hostility and dissolve grudges.

8. *Time project with the idea that you have better things to do with the rest of your life than scorching your mind about others' disfavors.* While you're at it, ask yourself how much what you're bitter about is going to matter as you move on with your life. See if the significance of what you're perturbing yourself about will be even more minimal as time passes.

9. *Vow to be fairer to yourself.* See that you're only hurting yourself as, while you're clinging to your angry, revenge,

grudge-filled fantasies, the other person isn't the least bit affected; that it is you who is hurt by your unforgiving ways.

10. *Get at your stubborn, pig-headed refusals to bury the hatchet any place but in the other person's head.* Basking in the false pride that is fueled by a bullheaded mentality may not be the best way to give yourself some emotional slack. Lightening up a little rather than tightening up a lot about misgivings you have about another's trespassing on your values might well be a more enjoyable way to live your nondress rehearsal of a life than you have.

11. *Emulate.* Look at the lives of others who are able to better roll with the punches rather than suffer in silence while grudgingly punching back. Ask them for the secret to their animosity removal success.

12. *Formally itemize the disadvantages of holding a grudge, from physical discomfort to loss of time spent on pet projects and general enjoyments.* Take 5 minutes each day to call to mind these minuses in a way that motivates you to more fully appreciate their handicaps en route to tacking on these revelations so as to lessen your begrudged tendencies.

13. *Talk nicely to others about those that you find generally disenchanting.* Rather than feed into your grudges by bad-mouthing those who have wronged you, pick out aspects of their personality and your experiences with them you have found favorable and communicate these to others - no matter how hard you are required to look for such flattery!

14. *Avoid the blame game to begin with.* Prevent grudges from forming to begin with by approaching life in a nonblaming fashion. Learn to expect and accept a fair amount of ill-advised treatment from others. That way you can prevent an inflation of your cantankerousness to begin with. The last item in this listing is a good road map to follow as you think more in ways that would better service your emotional well-being by resolving grudges before they start.

15. *Pick out those among these 16 suggestions that would be especially helpful for your use in curtailing your grudgeful tendencies.* Then, focus on using them, one at a time, each for a week at a time with the understanding that for each week you practice a chosen recommendation you reward yourself, for example, by going out for a meal at your favorite restaurant, going to a movie, or spending extra time in a sporting activity that you enjoy. Likewise, for each week that you fail to practice one of the helpful ideas you penalize yourself, for example, get up an hour earlier for a week, no dessert for a week, or no Saturday night out. This way you will have something positive to work toward and something negative to avoid while motivating yourself to becoming better able to keep a lid on your grudges.

16. *Challenge and change your beliefs from ill will to good will as follows:*

FROM	TO
• "I'll hang on to my spite if it kills me."	"Better that I loosen the grip of my spite so as to live freer and better."
• "Who does she think she is to wrong me in this utterly evil manner?"	"No matter who she thinks she is, she wronged me, and what is the point in wronging myself by holding a grudge?"
• "I'll show him who's boss by hating him forever and always."	"Better that I take charge of myself and be boss over my own hostility so that I can live more comfortably in the future."
• "I'll make her feel miserable by harboring a grudge - no matter how long it takes to rub it in."	"By harboring a grudge I'll only make myself feel miserable in no time flat."
• "I'll show him how much better I am than he is by dominating him with my grudges."	"If I live my life dominated by my grudges, I'll only make my life worse."

FROM *(Cont'd)*	TO *(Cont'd)*
• "I'll put on a grudge match that she won't soon forget."	"When I win a grudge match, I lose in the first round because it really is a form of self-punishment - punishing myself for the mistake of others."
• "If I don't hold a grudge, my enemy will boast that he beat me."	"If I do hold a grudge I'll have beaten myself, which is nothing to boast about."
• "Others will view me as weak if I don't walk around like I am going to deliver a knuckle sandwich to my opponent."	"Better that I strongly resolve to not walk around like a time bomb ready to go off."
• "How demeaning it is to act like nothing happened because of her disrespect. I must carry a grudge to prevent such negative evaluation."	"If I can accept myself in spite of others' disrespect toward me, there will be no basis for feeling demeaned nor desire to hold a grudge."
• "My pride is hurt and I have a right to show it by sticking to my grudgeful guns as if they were flypaper."	"I can only hurt my own pride by evaluating myself, giving myself a report card with a bad mark due to others' disfavors and disrespect directed toward me - and I've got better things to do than to use and abuse myself as a whipping post."

Holding grudges gives off illusions of power, magical thinking, sweet revenge, arrogance, self-righteousness, and a host of other self-defeating characteristics. Appreciate the realities that lie behind such fabrications so as to be more for yourself, even when under siege at times when others are acting against your best interests. Grudges can be made to go on indefinitely - if you let them. This chapter has presented a brainstorming of ideas that when practiced can assist in becoming well practiced in the art and science of limiting grudges that relate to others' limitations as expressed in their wrongful conduct toward you. Minimize grudge-filled resentment disguised as silent anger and see if by not extending that chip on your shoulder you are extending your chances for a happier, more pleasant existence;

that by ungluing that same chip you are not undoing a build-up of reams of harmful grudges. Don't begrudge yourself of the opportunity to do so!

Chapter 18 Review Questions

1. Why is self-pity one of the mechanics of holding a grudge?

2. How does pouting fit into the anatomy of begrudgedness?

3. From the chapter, what do you think is the best suggestion for removing the chip from one's shoulder that begrudgedness represents?

4. How are holding a grudge and magical thinking related?

5. How does time projection serve to lessen begrudgedness tendencies?

CHAPTER 19

The Reverse Golden Rule and How It Heads You in the Wrong, Hostile Direction

"Tit for tat, even Steven, fifty-fifty" is the often insistent call by people who believe they have extended themselves toward a happier relationship medium. One of the more common ideas constructed by humans is the reverse golden rule: "Others should do unto me as I do unto them, so because I'm nice and pleasant toward you and treat you with no lapses in kindness and consideration, you must likewise treat me with such similar good will - and you know what you are if you falter in doing so." This declaration of "If I'm nice to you, then, by George, by no strange coincidence, you have to be nice back to me" sounds good and reasonable enough; now if we could only get the world to run in orderly cycles it would actually have some practicality! In an ideal, balanced world such a seeming innocent request would do wonders for more peaceful relationships. Unfortunately, the universe runs randomly and impartially, and people in it are often not in a balanced frame of mind. Consequently, this demand for a return on one's investment of kindness doesn't hold water. In the end, staunch efforts to fit the round mythical reverse golden rule peg into a square reality hole creates more of the very problems it attempts to solve! By commanding that others, by cracky, better do unto you as you do unto them, you are declaring not a rule of thumb, but a law of the universe that:

1. *Has no basis in truth.* There is no evidence, save what you make up in your mind, that an equally favorable exchange is a given when making interpersonal contact. On the contrary, there are occasions when those you have frequently demonstrated that you care for the most will turn on you by treating you with ill-advised manners - and expect you to turn the other cheek to boot!

2. *Paves the way toward building up your own hostility.* If you expect, if not demand, an equal fair share of pleasantry and don't get it, you are liable to create resentment toward those who have emotionally and behaviorally short-changed you. This is more dramatically seen when you declare that you absolutely "NEED" or "MUST" have a return on your frequent and strong display of gentle acknowledgments of others.

3. *Creates other-blame and damnation.* If you believe the core requirement of this sacred rule, you are likely to conclude: "Because I need you to feed me the same honey that I feed you, rather than the vinegar that you are dishing out to me, you destroy me by depriving me of my necessities - you scum!" Need is short for necessity, and when such a lifeline is ruptured, there is the temptation to blame and condemn the one doing the depriving of alleged essentials.

4. *Promotes responsibility relapse.* In blaming other people for your emotional upset in the aftermath of their deficiencies of consideration, you imply, if not directly pronounce, that the deficient-acting caregiver is responsible for your emotions. "You antagonize me, make me, and cause me to feel upset when you don't trade off kindness for kindness (as you must)."

You can counter the tendency to establish a reverse, in reality not-so-golden rule by applying the following suggestions:

(a) *See the tarnish in the (golden) rule itself.* Recognize the folly of taking on such a demanding position to believe that significant others are required to be of like mind as you make it sound as if others have nothing else better to do than to follow your lead.

(b) *Distinguish preference from demand.* Understand and accept that though it may be desirable for others to join hands with you and aim for treating you more jovially, that doesn't mean that they have to do the "right" thing.

(c) *Rationally dispute with yourself.* Confront yourself with:

- "Where is the evidence that others must, are required to, treat me as I gently treat them?"
- "Why must I needlessly disturb myself by declaring it as horrendous when they don't latch on to my right-is-right theory?"
- "Where is the proof that my criticizer is bad for badly not returning my niceties?"

Then acknowledge that if you assert something to be true it is your responsibility as the asserter to prove its existence. Realize that there is no evidence to support the contention that others must treat you as you treat them, or the belief that it's catastrophic when they don't or that the offenders are evil for setting the stage for you offending yourself about their shortcomings in kindness.

(d) *Admit to a probable childish demand for reciprocation* (a return on your kind efforts). See that you likely invented this idea that "others should do unto me as I do unto them" as an infantile excuse to command others' return appreciations; that you fused and bonded ever so lovingly and pleasantly to this idea so that you could believe that you are entitled to a return of kindness. After all, how could someone you schemingly blanketed with kindness not administer the same toward you? "How dare he or she not be kind toward me!" Such relationship trickery is common with those who make themselves emotionally dependent on others' warmth, kindness, love, affection, and approval: "If I offer you droves of raving approval review, how could you possibly not do the same for poor little bitty old me?" Owning up to the facts of this balance-the-relationship game-playing budget so that I can gain some favor is a bitter pill to swallow, but it may strengthen the honesty and the guts of the relationship on the way down. Then:

(e) *Train yourself to be able to give favors with minimal expectations in return.* Lacking a hidden agenda, that is, "I'll show kindness toward you with the expectation that you will do the same toward me," will make for fewer hidden agendas cloaked in kindness and for less superficial and more authentic interactions with your social group.

(f) *Try not to "necessitize" or "essentialize."* Practice a nondemanding outlook that holds the prospect of taking pressure off yourself and your relationship with significant others. Believing that others' return of your pleasant attachments is nice but not necessary or essential can help in learning how to become a more tolerant, much less angry-acting person.

(g) *Appreciate individual difference.* See that certain others may not hold to the same kind of values as you. People you make an effort to be considerate toward may not have in their relationship arsenal the same appreciative streak that you do - nor must they.

(h) *Sort out nice from necessary.* Because something is good doesn't mean you have to be the recipient of it, including the brand of pleasantness that you may administer to others.

(i) *Challenge ideas that imply deservingness.* You get what you get, not what you want and think you deserve. Concluding that "because I treat others so well, I deserve to be treated well back" is rooted in illusion and self-pity.

(j) *Appreciate the fact that it takes a long time to find something that doesn't exist,* such as fairness generally and a fair exchange for your decent actions specifically. That way you will make yourself less blunted in the face of others' returning your kindness with antagonism.

(k) *Sort out disappointment from disaster.* Acknowledging rather than squelching or, at the other extreme, overreacting to disappointment is a tip-off to mental health. To feel disappointed when let down is to more fully appreciate your values, including the value of kindness being made into a two-way street. To tell yourself "How disappointing that my associate isn't being nice to me as I'm being nice to him" is a far cry from "How terrible that my associate treats me with such gigantic lapses in the kindness and consideration that I soak into her." Not exaggerating the significance of disappointment can greatly assist in not turning a mountain into a molehill.

(l) *Acknowledge others' free-will rather than your will.* The fact that others have a mind of their own and therefore can choose to thwart and balk your values, including your standard of evenmindedly not returning your good will with their sour will, is often overlooked in trying to figure out why you get treated so badly after treating others so well.

(m) *Challenge beholdingness notions.* Instead, pursue a philosophy of nonbeholdingness in others. Others are not beholden to you in mirroring your more positive approach to them. They can look at you, as a gift horse, in the mouth with no obligation to you to do otherwise.

(n) *Curtail inclinations to feel hurt.* Hurt is a weak, pathetic emotion that comes from self-blame and self-pity and is but two words away from anger; for example, "I feel hurt because of her critical actions - that bastard!"

(o) *Head self-pity off at the pass.* When betrayed by another's reversal of your consideration you may often be inclined to weepingly feel sorry for yourself. Such self-indulgent efforts prevent staying in tune with what can be done to do something with your time rather than stew away future opportunity.

(p) *Seize another's violation of this supposed law of the universe as an opportunity to fine-tune your emotional well-being.* By not damning the other and better tolerating the disappointing return from that person you can make something good out of something bad, without letting the bad overrule.

(q) Upon finding yourself feeling disenchantment due to others' limp-handed return of your fond efforts, *don't throw the baby out with the bath water* by declaring that because of your bad experience you will never meet anyone halfway again. Don't forsake the idea of pleasantly extending yourself to others just because you got a little mud in your eye from recent efforts to do so. Instead,

(r) *Vow to continue to act decently to others* - but for the right reasons; that is, hope that as you favorably reach out for them they will endear themselves back to you, but don't demand what you hope for. This is the general distinction between emotional sanity and emotional disturbance - desiring and actively seeking

your values, but not turning them into necessities/
demands. Continue to want, wish, prefer, desire, like,
and hope for people to evenly exchange kindness for
kindness; just don't make it a life-dependent value,
that is: "Others have to be nice to me upon my being
nice to them - and it's awful and they are awful when
they don't."

(s) *Don't retaliate.* Avoid a monkey-see, monkey-do,
get-even mentality. Don't take a bad situation and make
it worse by copying your ungrateful-acting associate's
antics. That way you remain true to yourself and help
to erase rather than race the flames of anger, hostility,
and vindictiveness.

(t) *Try to forge forgiveness and undamning acceptance
toward your adversaries' insensitivities.* Actively forgive rather than damn your colleagues for their motivational and/or ignorance limitations. They do not
have to be on the same trend or track as you, and it is
not helpful to get after them when they disappointingly
aren't.

(u) *Signal coping statements.* Have a roster of short but to
the point coping ideas that will snuff out tendencies
toward overreaction and taking personally disagreeing
conduct that goes against the grain of your gentle efforts. These include:

- "There is no reason why others have to act like me."
- "Demands lead to hostility, anger, and aggression -
  things I need about as much as a sore thumb."
- "Because I am not general manager of the universe,
  others and not I will dictate their response to me."
- "Erase, don't race, anger and animosity."
- "Others can do unto me as they choose to do unto
  me - not necessarily as I have done unto them."
- "Expect less, demand lesser yet."

- "Others have free-will and need not heed my will."
- "Everybody has their ways - and they are all different."
- "Nourish yourself when others don't."
- "When all else fails, you can treat yourself the way you would like to be treated."
- "When others treat you unfairly and unkindly, that is all the more reason to be fair and kind to yourself."
- "Don't take a bad situation and make it worse."
- "So far as I can tell, I'm not anointed to be the one person in the universe to always get fair returns on his emotional and relationship investments."
- "Fewer expectations lead to fewer disappointments and more frequent happiness."
- "I do not have to make myself beholden to others' returning my kindness in kind."
- "Disappointments are not disasters when people don't nicely frequent me as I frequently nicely frequent them."
- "Others are not bad when they badly neglect me in the face of my acceptance of them."
- "Condemn behaviors - not people."
- "My only choice in the whole matter is how much I am going to hassle myself and others about the way that they treat me."

Immediately after you fall or get pushed off the horse, get back on it. Return to your decent behavior standards toward others - but with a different mindset, one that allows for the possibility of an unbalanced return from your best relationship efforts. Put on your best face but with few expectations and with almost no demands for a return.

Final recommendation: Reverse the reverse golden rule and understand that others *don't* have to do unto you as you do unto them. See if you don't do yourself and your relationships with others a favor by reducing strain and ill will in you and toward others. By tarnishing the idea that others by your declaration and decree have to treat you nicely as you so do unto them, you make it more likely that by heading off at the pass this fairy tale expectation you are more likely to get yourself past relationship disappointments that will likely, due to individual differences of approach, continue to occur. Tarnishing the reverse golden rule can be made to have a way to make more clearly what and what not to realistically expect from others' treatment of you - with all the emotional and relationship advantages thereof.

Note. From *You Can Control Your Anger! 21 Ways To Do It* by Bill Borcherdt. Copyright © 2000, Professional Resource Exchange, Inc., P.O. Box 15560, Sarasota, FL 34277-1560.

Chapter 19 Review Questions

1. What is the definition of the alleged "reverse golden rule"?

2. Why is the reverse golden rule not an accurate portrayal of reality?

3. How does a belief in this concept discourage individual responsibility?

4. What is a demand for reciprocation and where does it get you?

5. Why is learning the ability to give with no expectation for return important?

CHAPTER 20

Force-Feeding Constructive Ideas and Their Destructive Outcomes

Good suggestions, like good intentions, are not always backed by the right methods. However helpful advice might turn out to be, such potential positive outcomes can be dashed by a roughshod approach to helping that may have the net effect of others retaliating against your force-feeding ways. Practically anything good carried to its extreme is likely to reverse its positive effects. The sun feels good, but if you stay out in it long enough you are likely to get a sunburn; you may enjoy your job, but if you work to excess your work may lose its positive flavor; you may thrive on being a parent, but if you are with your kids too much you might put a damper on some of your zest for associating with them. This chapter will demonstrate why and how otherwise constructive suggestions, if fanatically forced upon others, are likely to create self-defeating outcomes. Reasons for such forcefulness and what can be done by both the sender and receiver of such conspicuous outcomes will be reviewed.

"I've come across the truth and I simply cannot understand why the rest of the world isn't eager to hear what it is," is the implied battle cry of those who try to force-feed their values onto and into others. One of the most difficult things for humans to understand and accept is how anyone can have a different view of the world than they. The greater the distinction, the more difficulty the acceptance of the wavelength gap. Furthermore, in the aftermath of such a values discrepancy, the force-feeder often foolishly concludes, "If I get angry enough at those who refuse to buy into what I know to be the truth, I'll use my anger as an agent of control to sway them in my direction and toward my directives." This charge in the form of a demand that "Others must accept my ideas and I must force them upon those that ignorantly refuse to abide by them" will likely dissolve the good will of most relationships. To angrily force-feed others defeats the purposes of more rational living, which is to live more harmoniously and to be happier, within the context of our social group. The remainder of the chapter will be divided into three parts: (a) examples of destructive outcomes in response to attempted ramming of one's ideas down another's throat, (b) new ways of looking at old force-feeding problems in the form of vigorously ripping up the demanding thinking that propels such ideas of "swallow my ideas and ideals or else," and (c) ways one can protect oneself from nonsensical-acting force-feeders short of putting a gun to their head; in other words, how to use your noodle when others around you are losing theirs - and are blaming you for their loss!

Part I

Following is a series of destructive outcomes that may follow even well-intended efforts that begin with helpful efforts to persuade others along the lines of an idea that you believe would be potentially profitable to them, but are made to end with you going from suggested helpfulness to demanding force-fulness.

1. *Good ideas getting lost in the shuffle due to insistences that they be adopted.* Others are likely to pay more attention to your zealous manner and rampaging style rather than the content of your message. Your overemotional appeals are likely to drown out the good news that lies beside them.
2. *Social group avoidance.* When it comes to feeding time, there may be no one around who will listen. After all, who wants to be around someone who nags and acts like a porcupine or a demander. The world can be a lonely place when one is embroiled in self-righteous conduct.
3. *Frenzy, fanaticism, and bigotry are rehearsed.* Closed-mindedness is further cemented by displays of fervor that strengthen preexisting righteous indignation. The more forcibly you do something, the stronger the effects of your efforts, even when what you are forcefully trying to do isn't good for you.
4. *Loss of love and other intimate relationships.* Often, the more love and concern one has for another the harder the attempt to make the cared-for one happy - but only in ways that the caretaker approves of! In the wake of a mentality of "Because I love you so much I know what is better for you more than you do," the one being forced upon may sense the relationship eroding, leading to a falling out of love and eventually exiting the relationship. The force-feeder may end up scratching his or her head while wondering, "Where did I go wrong? I was only trying to help."
5. *Increases feelings of insecurity reflected in the insistent notion "Be reasonable - view it my way."* This suggestion implies the absolute necessity of being right, lest I become even more of an inferior person for not being able to convince others to buy into my frame of reference. "What is wrong with me that I can't get others to take upon my valued ideas?" infers a feeling of inferiority to begin with and the other's refusal to adopt your mandates as an avenue for expressing such preexisting feelings of feebleness.

6. *Crushes workable compromising possibilities.* Lavish ideas designed to beautify another's life aren't so pretty when insisted upon in that they leave no room for compromise. "One way," "my way," "the way," and "the only way" present a mechanical view of options that leaves no possibilities for meeting someplace in between with alternatives. Other possibilities are stifled; the hardest thing to give - in - rigidly remains in place.

7. *Builds self-defeating entitlement philosophies.* Entitlement notions, mainly "Everyone is entitled to my opinion," maintain a fixed position; consequently, permissiveness and emotional slack are weakened to the demise of smoother, better lubricated peer and family relationships.

8. *Often results in being passed by rather than receiving resources and opportunities that would allow for a fuller, more enriching, more enjoyable life.* Force yourself upon others and they will likely boycott providing you when it comes time for them to provide you with goods, services, and promotions that would allow for a more convenient, happier life.

9. *Further activates the fear of being wrong.* For many, being wrong is viewed almost as a fate worse than death. The faulty notion that you are dealing from a weakened position when admitting wrongdoing locks in your faults indefinitely in that until a philosophy of admittance is established what is wrong will likely never be made right.

10. *Disrespects individual differences.* Feuds, conflicts, and mutual antagonisms of various passive-aggressive or outright aggressive vintage are likely to be put into play when one person tries to tattoo his or her demands and commands upon another. Disrespect for conflicting values promotes warlike avenues of hostile expression.

11. *Often ends with assorted irrational attempts to prove oneself rather than more rationally be oneself.* The more intense the command that another buy into what one is offering, the more a self-proving power struggle is likely

to be unraveled. Taking refusal to purchase your values personally often results in a bottomless pit of an effort to do the impossible of proving yourself.

Part II

New ways of looking at old force-feeding problems by countering and ripping up the demanding thoughts that fuel fanatical efforts to make others over.

THOUGHTS THAT BREED FORCE-FEEDING AND CAUSE EMOTIONAL INDIGESTION	COUNTERING SELF-INSTRUCTIONAL MESSAGES THAT DON'T HASSLE OTHERS WHO DIGEST THEIR OWN CHOSEN IDEAS AND DECISIONS
• "Others must feast upon my suggestions - or else."	"Others have a choice as to whether they eat what I attempt to feed them. My choice is whether it would be advisable to hassle them about their decision."
• "I know what's best for him, even more so than he."	"Who am I trying to kid? Because he has lived with himself for a lifetime, he knows much more about himself than I ever will."
• "I'll force what's best for her down her throat - she'll thank me later."	"If I try to force-feed her ideas, she is likely to resent me later."
• "He needs help and I need to provide it."	"He can use some help in struggling by himself so he can learn from his efforts."
• "There's no room for compromise here; she must see and do it my way."	"Better that I leave margin for error in both our positions, especially since we are dealing with not one, but two humans."
• "I can predict what is going to be best for him."	"A crystal ball have I not. I can predict all right - about as accurately as an astrologer's forecast."

THOUGHTS THAT BREED FORCE-FEEDING AND CAUSE EMOTIONAL INDIGESTION *(Cont'd)*	COUNTERING SELF-INSTRUCTIONAL MESSAGES THAT DON'T HASSLE OTHERS WHO DIGEST THEIR OWN CHOSEN IDEAS AND DECISIONS *(Cont'd)*
• "What's wrong with me that I can't persuade her toward my version of the truth, which is really *the* version?"	"There's nothing wrong with me because people march to the tune of their own drummer rather than listening to my drumbeats."
• "My way is the way!"	"My way is my way and not her way, and perhaps, just perhaps, never the twain shall meet."
• "I'll push until my ideas sink in."	"If I keep pushing, my efforts will likely backfire because he will likely pull at the polar opposite to my pushing."
• "Anyone and everyone should realize that this is a stellar idea."	"She isn't just anyone or everyone; she is different from both myself and the masses. I'd best honor rather than disrespect her divergent views."

Part III

How to protect oneself when on the receiving end of non-sensical-acting force-feeders. When the shoe is on the other foot and you are forced to cope with force-feeders, consider the following philosophical and practical suggestions designed to nondefensively patronize and protect yourself from the potential emotional indigestion related to wrestling with such antagonists.

1. *Acknowledge the other's feelings; don't get bogged down in their content.* Patronizing statements such as "I can tell you have given this topic a lot of thought," "I admire the strength of your convictions," and "You really feel strongly about that, don't you" are constructive ways of deflecting destructive demands.

2. *Thanks but no thanks.* Acknowledge appreciation for the other's interest in you but be quick to explain that you prefer to figure out solutions to your current life circumstances on your own.
3. *Blend in with the flow of the force-feeding attack rather than meet it head on.* Find some truth, some shades of gray in what the other is evangelistically saying. It's harder to stalk someone who acknowledges as truth some aspect of your philosophy.
4. *Establish undamning acceptance of others.* Accept others with their fervor lest you become like others in feverishly protesting against them and their ways.
5. *Dig in your heels so as to pave the way for your own low frustration tolerance (LFT) improvements.* Don't exaggerate the difficulty of putting up with obnoxious conduct in another or you may get yourself quite emotionally winded.
6. *View your antagonist as your helper.* By coping with fanaticism with all its steam you are supporting your own mental health improvements, not only now but in future encounters with contrary-acting people.
7. *Understand that if it were not you as the target of such antagonistic conduct, it would be someone else.* The force-feeder is treating you in the same way that he or she would treat anyone who differed from him or her. Appreciating this random factor is an encouragement to not personalize others' ill-advised ways.
8. *If necessary, agree with them if that's what it takes to ease their force-feed-without-ceasing philosophy.* Taking the line of least resistance is sometimes more advisable.
9. *Drum up an escape clause.* When finding it especially difficult to remove yourself from their presence, make up a white lie that permits you to exit the premises and their presence, such as, "My mate is expecting me to pick him/her up 5 minutes ago" even though you have no mate!

10. *Sharp flattery can separate you from another's provocations; for example, "Your ideas are some of the most unusual and interesting that I have ever encountered on the subject."* Such staged performances can assist at keeping others at arm's length while deflecting their annoying antics.

11. *Give yourself unconditional self-acceptance (USA).* This thorough suggestion, as the best of them all, was saved for last. By accepting yourself in spite of others' outlandish behavior, you keep others' attempts to ruffle your emotions at bay. Defining others' conduct, but not defining yourself by it, allows you to not be taken advantage of while not judging yourself by others' difficult behavior. The misery equation "Others' conduct equals me" can be avoided in favor of "Others' conduct reflects their values but does not represent me."

Will Rogers said, "The thing that we do worse than any other nation is to manage somebody else's affairs." Whether attempting to force-feed local values on nations or an individual's values on another person, the destructive result is practically always the same. Most people have a resistance to being told what to do with force-feeders who imply that they know more about you than you. Strong backlash often follows insistences that "I know better." It would be better for the sometimes good intentions to be backed by the right methods by simply minding one's own business. By being constructive in not offering unsolicited suggestions you avoid the destruction that often follows otherwise well-intended, constructive tactics. Instead of creating problems by forcefully trying to manage others' affairs, allow them the leisure of feeding themselves at their own pace and in their own way. That way you will prevent emotional and relationship indigestion outcomes.

Note. From *You Can Control Your Anger! 21 Ways To Do It* by Bill Borcherdt. Copyright © 2000, Professional Resource Exchange, Inc., P.O. Box 15560, Sarasota, FL 34277-1560.

Chapter 20 Review Questions

1. How can anger prevent good intentions from joining with the right methods?

2. Why does insistence that others believe like you sabotage your efforts to persuade them?

3. Why does force-feeding destroy compromise possibilities?

4. How does the fear of being wrong explain force-feeding as a problem?

5. What do you think is the best way to protect yourself from being on the receiving end of a force-feeding-acting person?

CHAPTER 21

Missiling and Misleading Yourself by the Short-Range Advantages of Anger While Missing Out on All the Long-Range Fun

Anger expression feels good and Godlike in the short run, but what is often overlooked is its long-range disadvantages. This chapter attempts to correct this common oversight so as to give not just pleasure-of-the-moment perspective to this powerful emotion, but also to balance such frivolity with the pain later on. True, you can shoot the angry works today and immediately feel better, but you will suffer an emotional interpersonal hangover tomorrow due to your outbursts putting you at odds with your social group. As Mark Twain said, "Speak when you're angry and you will make the best speech that you will ever regret." Anger is like acid in that it will eventually destroy the container that holds it. Due to its immediate "feel-good" effects, individuals, nations, groups, tribes, and so on, mislead themselves into believing that anger is a good thing rather than perhaps the most destructive of all mood states. When contemplating anger build-up and/or expression, readers are encouraged to stop and ask themselves, "Do I want to feel better right now by spewing out my righteous indignation, or do I want to feel better for the rest of my life by building a case for unangry, tolerant restraint?" By choosing the latter alternative of flinching less in the face of injustice, you are accepting the short-run sacrifices of immediate restraint for the long-range gains that accompany the feelings of accomplishment that come from developing yourself into a more tolerant, accepting human being. Tolerance and acceptance won't guarantee a life filled with more fun, but it is unlikely that you will have much fun without it - just ask the person who just completed the best speech he or she will ever regret!

Short-range pleasure and immediate gratification have appealing qualities that if worshipped enough can be cemented into addictive qualities. Gratification and indulgence are made to replace restraint and patience. Pleasure is gained while perspective is lost in the sea of tunnel-visioned anger. Today's gains are spent in anger expression, while tomorrow's pains are yet to come. To avoid this long-range negative fate, lead yourself not into temptation as it will find you. When you have the temptation to "go off" with your anger, see that there is less pain in restraining your anguish than there is in expressing it. Visualize and explain to yourself in no-nonsense fashion that it is not easy to take the easy way out and that the present strain of restraint is but a small price to pay for the hopeful possibilities that can accrue from emotional self-control.

Testing out such long-range hypotheses will require you to look beyond your own nose via a down-the-road view. This is not an easy exercise to master in that humans naturally seem to believe that it's easier to go with the flow of emotions than to restrain them. In the immediate flow of anger, yes! In the long-range and overall scheme of your happiness and survival, no! Long-range comfort of anger restraint competes with some of the immediate short-term benefits of anger expression that I will list. Whether the short-run or long-run gains are made to dominate will largely be determined by how well you have allowed yourself to be educated on the value of looking at your conduct and more rationally determine its effects upon you over the course of a lifetime. First, I will review why the creation and/or expression of anger is often viewed as an item based on immediate comfort and instant convenience; then, I will list some direct suggestions for overcoming missiling and misleading tendencies:

1. *Lusting after self-esteem enhancement.* People in this country have gotten themselves preoccupied with skyrocketing their self-esteem. All worried about esteeming or rating themselves as high, many desperately do whatever is the quickest thing to do to measure themselves in a favorable way. Measuring of self has become perhaps the favorite indoor and outdoor sport for most Americans. Perhaps the most accessible way to esteem yourself is to make yourself blisteringly angry and hostile toward someone. That way you will feel superhuman, if not like God Almighty, that you're so much better than the person that you are angrily looking down upon. Such a devoted attachment to a holier-than-thou belief system immediately renders a powerful feeling that, a split second ago, had been a powerless feeling state.

2. *Combats boredom.* Anger gives an otherwise drab-feeling person an instant exciting boost. For all its long-range drawbacks, in the short run anger expression can be exciting. Such energy-producing outbursts can quicken one's emotional pace and liven up an otherwise humdrum existence.

3. *Fights depression.* If you quickly blame someone else you can skirt the notion of blaming yourself. Not that somebody is required to be blamed for a wrongdoing, but if one sees self-blame as causing depression, this can be quickly sidestepped by pointing a finger at someone else as the alleged bad guy. Beating on someone is more convenient and comfortable than beating upon yourself.

4. *As an attempt to impress others.* The boisterous drama that often accompanies anger can be a feeble attempt to impress your social group as to your seeming potency. (Im)-

potency is instead revealed in the long run when associates discover that what lies behind your mask of strength is really fear and insecurity that others will not think well of you unless you theatrically impress them with an anger extravaganza.

5. *Illusions of conquest.* Getting the best of another by forcing them to say uncle by acknowledging your rightness and their wrongness is a sorry sight but yet a convenient method of establishing domination. Such acts of one-ups-personship reflect a cover-up for lack of self-confidence. These illusions, when taking on a life of their own, provide the immediate smug sense of satisfaction that comes from living life in the fast fantasy lane. Triumphant outbursts, though temporarily satisfying, usually lead to ongoing, long-term conflicts with one's social group.

6. *Has addictive hurrah components.* Though anger immediately and dramatically feels good, it's bad for you. This is due in part to the addictive longing that humans often have to go back to practically anything that feels good, even when it has a long-range destructive component to it. Anger with its lethal potential fits that category.

7. *Instigates immediate assertive, disinhibited action.* Anger as nerve gas often starts out with the excitement of striving for what you want and ends by aggressively running roughshod over anyone who wants something different. Anger unleashes energy of the type that you can do without when trying to motivate yourself. There is nothing you can do with anger that you can't do without it - besides kill someone!

8. *Can serve as a quick substitute for hurt.* Hurt takes the emotional wind out of one's sails; it feels weak, impotent, and lifeless. Anger, on the other hand, is a feeling you can hang your hat on. During its expression, one feels full of life, if not Godlike. Hurt has a mysterious ring to it; anger has a dramatic flair to it. Weak feelings can be quickly

substituted by more energetic anger, and often are. Blaming another for your hurt feelings, that is, "You hurt me, you bastard," quickly transposes the emptiness of hurt to the fullness of anger. Emptied of hurt, anger is then free to dismantle who and whatever thwarts gaining what the angry-acting person is insisting upon.

9. *Excuses not working toward the emotional stamina necessary to develop patience.* Letting emotional debris angrily multiply justifies not giving peace and higher frustration tolerance a chance. Going downstream with the current of anger seems easier at the moment than fighting upstream against it. Emotional stamina-building opportunity is lost by giving way to the short-run comforts that anger expression has to offer.

10. *Can gain others' immediate attention while playing upon their vulnerabilities.* Anger provides an emotional splurge that is like no other, and sometimes it allows you to get what you want from others in no time flat. Others intimidating themselves in the face of your anger often results in others fearfully giving way to your way. The immediate advantageous effects of anger are strengthened by others displaying their vulnerability toward your emotional splurges.

11. *Presents physical sensation contrasts that can temporarily provide a soothing effect that can establish a method of relaxation.* Anger build-up leads to physical tension, and if such stress is followed by an expressively letting out of the hot air build-up, immediate comfort is gained from this depressurization. The individual *feels* better from the tension build-up to relaxation journey but doesn't *get* better in that the philosophical manner of creating the original anger is not made to matter. In fact, the physical comforts from building up and releasing stress and anger are strengthened in the practice of this cycle. Clenched fists, grinding teeth, tightness in various bodily areas, and churning in the stomach are often followed by a relaxed

state once the anger subsides. However, churning leads to a returning of the anger in that its core cause, demanding thinking, goes untouched.

12. *Provides for intoxication without drugs.* Angry-acting people in all their fervor experience a drunken state of mind that takes them gleefully past a more natural and neutral state of consciousness. When my son was 6, I was spinning him around and around on his toboggan under the street light in Wisconsin's wintertime. After several revolutions I stopped and, as Billy tipsily got off the toboggan, he said "I'm high!" Anger with all its intensity can provide for a glorified state of mind that is mind altering.

13. *Provokes arrogance and feelings of superiority with all its "holier-than-thou" immediate amenities that perfume underlying "unworthier-than-all" fears and insecurities.*

Suggestions to avoid opting for the more immediate emotional chill and temporary practical advantages of flying off the handle, only to land in a self-defeating position, include:

(a) *Fill yourself up with heavy doses of consequential thinking in terms of reminding yourself where anger has (not) gotten you, your social group, or the world generally.* Then,

(b) *Apply confrontive self-questions:*

- "Where does my thinking get me?"
- "What would be a better way to look at this matter?"
- "Why would I want to associate with a wounded animal?"
- "Do I want to feel better right now by blowing off steam, or do I want to feel better for the rest of my life by molding myself into a more tolerant human being?"
- "Looking at my track record, what will harm me more, less or more restraint?"

- "Judging from the world happenings as seen on the front page of my newspaper, does more harm come from restraint or lack of restraint?"
- "Restraint is not a dirty word - unangry restraint, that is."
- "Is it the situation or my thinking about the situation that creates my anger?"
- "How can I help myself to better see that people are going to be the way they are, not the way I would like them to be?"
- "Why do not others have a right to purposefully, intentionally, and willfully trespass all over my values?"

(c) *Anticipate angry upsets as taking a bad situation and making it worse.* Realize that anger is like throwing gasoline on a campfire with all the campers within range of the heat rage getting hurt.

(d) *Track down magical thinking.* When not in an angry frame of mind, consider that when you put yourself in an angry state you believe that your anger frenzy will somehow change matters and people of concern. This will definitely be the case - change toward the worse, that is.

(e) *Contest the idea that your values are superior.* Just because what you stand for is different from what others believe does not mean that your ideas are holy and that theirs are sinister. A sense of humility can go a long way toward better lubricating your relationships with your social group as well as toward dissolving anger.

(f) *View restraint as a small price to pay for getting a better grip on your angry feelings.* Restraint breeds tolerance and patience which is a real advantage when understanding that many problems in the world stem from lack of restraint. What the world can use more is more, not less, restraint of anger expressions.

(g) *Appreciate that anger is a poor way to express a message.* Express yourself when you are angry and you will make the best expression you will ever regret. The best-intended message will get lost in the anger expression shuffle by the manner in which you deliver your angry (punch) lines. Listeners will likely pick up on your emotional steam to the neglect of the ideas you wish to communicate.

(h) *Think about the future, specifically the disadvantages of being associated with a wounded animal.* Others who do not take kindly to your angry approach may pick their future spots in attempting their own brand of bittersweet revenge, turning sour on their relationship with you. It is no fun sharing space with someone who is hell bent on retaliation and antagonism.

(i) *Make the acceptance shoe fit the other foot.* Instead of declaring to yourself, "He/She should know better by now," reframe that demand into accepting your responsibility for changing by telling yourself, "It would be better that I know and accept by now that my adversary is unlikely to change a lick and that therefore it would be far better for me to save the emotional wear and tear that comes from me foolishly expecting him or her to!"

(j) *Understand that your vindictive-acting associate is representing his or her values and is not near as much against you as it appears.* Hostility can be neutralized and taking matters personally can be diminished by underscoring this no-harm-intended idea. A huge majority of humans don't have the time to purposefully do us in, but will often take the time to express the values that are important to them.

Something is missing when you mislead yourself into focusing mainly on the sometimes immediate advantages of anger and its expression. This chapter points to a finer appreciation of the longer range advantages of taking a no-nonsense, forthright, directly educational, rational approach to being realistic and honest with yourself when tallying up the pros and cons of anger development and expressions. What is missing in the misguided and misleading short-range equation is a fuller understanding of the embittered emotional fallout that has, as its main consequence, a missing out on all of the long-range fun.

Chapter 21 Review Questions

1. How is anger advantageous in the short run?

2. How are dire needs for approval and anger linked?

3. How is anger an intimidation factor in relationships?

4. How can confrontive self-questions apply to anger control?

5. How can contesting that your values are superior encourage anger control?

Bibliography

Alberti, R. E. (1990). *Stand Up, Speak Out, Talk Back*. San Luis Obispo, CA: Impact.

Alberti, R. E., & Emmons, M. L. (1975). *Stand Up, Speak Out, Talk Back!* New York: Pocket Books.

Alberti, R. E., & Emmons, M. L. (1990). *Your Perfect Right: A Guide to Assertive Living* (6th ed.). San Luis Obispo, CA: Impact.

Bach, G. R., & Wyden, P. (1968). *The Intimate Enemy*. New York: Avon.

Becker, W. C. (1971). *Parents Are Teachers*. Champaign, IL: Research Press.

Bell, N. W., & Vogel, E. F. (1965). *The Family*. New York: The Free Press.

Bernard, M. E., & Joyce, M. R. (1984). *Rational-Emotive Therapy With Children and Adolescents*. New York: John Wiley and Sons.

Borcherdt, B. (1989). *Think Straight! Feel Great! 21 Guides to Emotional Self-Control*. Sarasota, FL: Professional Resource Exchange.

Borcherdt, B. (1993). *You Can Control Your Feelings: 24 Guides to Emotional Well-Being*. Sarasota, FL: Professional Resource Press.

Borcherdt, B. (1996a). *Head Over Heart in Love: 25 Guides to Rational Passion.* Sarasota, FL: Professional Resource Press.

Borcherdt, B. (1996b). *Fundamentals of Cognitive-Behavior Therapy: From Both Sides of the Desk.* New York: Haworth Press.

Borcherdt, B. (1996c). *Making Families Work and What to Do When They Don't.* New York: Haworth Press.

Borcherdt, B. (1998). *Feeling Right When Things Go Wrong.* Sarasota, FL: Professional Resource Press.

Buntman, P. H. (1979). *How to Live With Your Teen-Ager.* Pasadena, CA: The Birch Tree Press.

Dobson, J. (1996). *The New Dare to Discipline.* Wheaton, IL: Tyndale House Publishing.

Dryden, W. (1990). *Dealing With Anger Problems: Rational-Emotive Therapeutic Interventions.* Sarasota, FL: Professional Resource Exchange.

Dryden, W. (1991). *A Dialogue With Albert Ellis: Against Dogma.* Philadelphia, PA: Open University Press.

Dryden, W., & DiGiuseppe, R. (1990). *A Primer on Rational-Emotive Therapy.* San Jose, CA: Resource Press.

Dryden, W., & Golden, W. L. (1987). *Cognitive-Behavioral Approaches to Psychotherapy.* Bristol, PA: Hemisphere Publishing.

Edelstein, M. R., & Steele, D. R. (1998). *The Three Minute Therapy: Change Your Thinking, Change Your Life.* Lakewood, CO: Glenbridge Publishing LTD.

Ellis, A. (1961). *A Guide to a Successful Marriage.* N. Hollywood, CA: Wilshire Book Company.

Ellis, A. (1965). *Suppressed: 7 Key Essays Publishers Dared Not Print.* Chicago, IL: New Classics House.

Ellis, A. (1966a). *The Art and Science of Love.* Secaucus, NJ: Lyle Stuart.

Ellis, A. (1966b). *How to Raise an Emotionally Healthy, Happy Child.* N. Hollywood, CA: Wilshire Book Company.

Ellis, A. (1971). *Growth Through Reason*. N. Hollywood, CA: Wilshire Book Company.

Ellis, A. (1972a). *The Civilized Couples Guide to Extra-Marital Affairs*. New York: Peter H. Wyden.

Ellis, A. (1972b). *The Sensuous Person: Critique and Corrections*. Secaucus, NJ: Lyle Stuart.

Ellis, A. (1974). *Humanistic Psychotherapy*. New York: McGraw-Hill.

Ellis, A. (1975). *How to Live With a Neurotic at Home and Work*. New York: Crown Publishers.

Ellis, A. (1979a). *The Intelligent Woman's Guide to Dating and Mating*. Secaucus, NJ: Lyle Stuart.

Ellis, A. (1979b). *Overcoming Procrastination*. New York: Signet.

Ellis, A. (1979c). *Reason and Emotion in Psychotherapy*. Secaucus, NJ: The Citadel Press.

Ellis, A. (1982). *Rational Assertiveness Training* (Audiotape). New York: Institute for Rational Living.

Ellis, A. (1988). *How to Stubbornly Refuse to Make Yourself Miserable About Anything - Yes, Anything!* Secaucus, NJ: Lyle Stuart.

Ellis, A. (1991). *Why Am I Always Broke: How to be Sure About Money*. New York: Carol Publishing.

Ellis, A., & Abrahms, E. (1978). *Brief Psychotherapy in Medical and Health Practice*. New York: Springer.

Ellis, A., & Becker, I. (1982). *A Guide to Personal Happiness*. N. Hollywood, CA: Wilshire Book Company.

Ellis, A., & Harper, R. (1975). *A New Guide to Rational Living*. N. Hollywood, CA: Wilshire Book Company.

Ellis, A., & Tafrate, R. C. (1998). *How to Control Your Anger Before It Controls You*. Secaucus, NJ: Carol Publishing.

Ellis, A., & Whiteley, J. (1979). *Theoretical and Empirical Foundation of Rational-Emotive Therapy*. Monterey, CA: Brooks/Cole.

Ellis, A., & Yeager, R. J. (1989). *Why Some Therapies Don't Work: The Dangers of Transpersonal Psychology*. Buffalo, NY: Prometheus Books.

Fensterheim, H., & Baer, J. (1977). *Don't Say Yes When You Want to Say No*. New York: Dell.

Fraiberg, S. H. (1959). *The Magic Years*. New York: Charles Scribner's Sons.

Frankl, V. E. (1959). *Man's Search for Meaning*. New York: Touchstone Books.

Garcia, E. (1979). *Developing Emotional Muscle*. Atlanta: Author.

Garner, A. (1981). *Conversationally Speaking*. New York: McGraw-Hill.

Glasser, W. (1975). *Reality Therapy*. New York: Harper Colophon Books.

Greenberg, D. (1966). *How to Make Yourself Miserable*. New York: Random House.

Greiger, R. M., & Boyd, J. D. (1980). *Rational-Emotive Therapy: A Skills Based Approach*. New York: Van Nostrand Reinhold.

Grossack, M. (1976). *Love, Sex, and Self-Fulfillment*. New York: Signet.

Haley, J., & Hoffman, L. (1967). *Techniques of Family Therapy*. New York: Basic Books.

Harris, S. (1982). *Pieces of Eight*. Boston: Houghton Mifflin.

Hauck, P. (1971). *Marriage Is a Loving Business*. Philadelphia, PA: The Westminster Press.

Hauck, P. (1974). *Overcoming Frustration and Anger*. Philadelphia, PA: The Westminster Press.

Hauck, P. (1976). *How to Do What You Want to Do*. Philadelphia, PA: The Westminster Press.

Hauck, P. (1978). *Overcoming Depression*. Philadelphia, PA: The Westminster Press.

Hauck, P. (1981). *Overcoming Jealousy and Possessiveness*. Philadelphia, PA: The Westminster Press.

Hauck, P. (1984). *The Three Faces of Love*. Philadelphia, PA: The Westminster Press.

Hoffer, E. (1966). *The True Believer*. New York: Perennial Library.

Holt, J. (1970a). *How Children Fail*. New York: Dell.

Holt, J. (1970b). *How Children Learn*. New York: Dell.

James, M., & Jongeward, D. (1973). *Born to Win*. Reading, PA: Addison-Wesley.

Johnson, W. R. (1981). *So Desperate the Fight*. New York: Institute for Rational Living.

Jourard, S. (1971). *The Transparent Self*. New York: D. Van Nostrand.

Lazarus, A. A. (1981). *The Practice of Multi-Modal Therapy*. New York: McGraw-Hill.

Lazarus, A. A. (1984). *In the Minds Eye: The Power of Imagery for Personal Enrichment*. New York: Guilford.

Lazarus, A. A. (1985). *Marital Myths: Two Dozen Mistaken Beliefs That Can Ruin a Marriage (or Make a Bad One Worse)*. San Luis Obispo, CA: Impact.

Lazarus, A. A. (1989). *The Practice of Multimodal Therapy: Systematic, Comprehensive and Effective Psychotherapy*. Johns Hopkins.

Lazarus, A. A., & Fay, A. (1975). *I Can If I Want to*. New York: Warner Books.

Maultsby, M. (1975). *Help Yourself to Happiness*. New York: Institute for Rational Living.

Meichenbaum, D. (1977). *Cognitive-Behavior Modification: An Integrative Approach*. New York: Plenum.

Paris, C., & Casey, B. (1979). *Project: You, a Manual of Rational Assertiveness Training*. Portland, OR: Bridges Press.

Paterson, G. R. (1978). *Families*. Champaign, IL: Research Press.

Perls, F. S. (1969). *In and Out of the Garbage Pail*. New York: Bantam Books.

Putney, S., & Putney, G. J. (1966). *The Adjusted American: Normal Neuroses in the Individual and Society.* New York: Harper Colophon Books.

Reisman, D. (1962). *The Lonely Crowd.* New Haven: Yale University Press.

Russell, B. (1971). *The Conquest of Happiness.* New York: Liveright.

Russianoff, P. (1983). *Why Do I Think I'm Nothing Without a Man?* New York: Bantam Books.

Satir, V. (1967). *Conjoint Family Therapy.* Palo Alto, CA: Science and Behavior Books.

Satir, V. (1972). *Peoplemaking.* Palo Alto, CA: Science and Behavior Books.

Shedd, C. W. (1978). *Smart Dads I Know.* New York: Avon.

Simon, S. B. (1978). *Negative Criticism and What You Can Do About It.* Niles, IL: Argus Communications.

Smith, M. J. (1975). *When I Say No, I Feel Guilty.* New York: Bantam Books.

Walen, S. R., DiGiuseppe, R., & Wessler, R. L. (1980). *A Practitioner's Guide to Rational-Emotive Therapy.* New York: Oxford University Press.

Weeks, C. (1981). *Simple, Effective Treatment of Agoraphobia.* New York: Bantam Books.

Young, H. S. (1974). *A Rational Counseling Primer.* New York: Institute for Rational Living.

Zilbergeld, B. (1978). *Male Sexuality.* Boston, MA: Little, Brown, and Company.

Zilbergeld, B. (1983). *The Shrinking of America: Myths of Psychological Change.* Boston, MA: Little, Brown, and Company.

Zilbergeld, B. (1992). *The New Male Sexuality.* New York: Bantam Books.

Zilbergeld, B., & Lazarus, A. A. (1988). *Mindpower: Getting What You Want Through Mental Training.* New York: Ivy Books.